Chip & I,

May God continue in your efforts to be a light for him in all your endeavors. May your story resonate with many.

Kermo

April 9, 2018

When God Speaks...
Will You Hear?

Kerusso

WESTBOW
PRESS®
A DIVISION OF THOMAS NELSON
& ZONDERVAN

Scripture taken from the Holy Bible, NEW INTERNATIONAL VERSION®. Copyright © 1973, 1978, 1984, 2011 by Biblica, Inc. All rights reserved worldwide. Used by permission. NEW INTERNATIONAL VERSION® and NIV® are registered trademarks of Biblica, Inc. Use of either trademark for the offering of goods or services requires the prior written consent of Biblica US, Inc.

WestBow Press books may be ordered through booksellers or by contacting:

WestBow Press
A Division of Thomas Nelson & Zondervan
1663 Liberty Drive
Bloomington, IN 47403
www.westbowpress.com
1 (866) 928-1240

ISBN: 978-1-5127-3261-0 (sc)
ISBN: 978-1-5127-3262-7 (hc)
ISBN: 978-1-5127-3260-3 (e)

Library of Congress Control Number: 2016903253

Print information available on the last page.

WestBow Press rev. date: 02/26/2016

This is dedicated to the hurting people and the lost people who are tired of living in an upside down world and who seek something better in life. May you know that God is speaking to you even now!

Prelude

I invite you into the middle of a story, a story in which the ending has yet to be written. Does this strike you as strange? You may wonder who would start a story in the middle and then not tell the ending, but is this not the way of most stories? Our lives are individual stories that unfold day by day. Each day brings the turning of a page as we write of new experiences and adventures. We turn the pages of our lives and move seamlessly from one chapter to the next, but we never know what is on the next page until we live it. When we meet someone, we typically enter into the middle of their story. We are rarely there at the beginning and usually not at the end. We may know nothing of what has gone before or what will happen next. We know neither the beginning nor the end, only the middle part that we are allowed to enter for that moment in time. That is why I invite you into the middle of a story, because I cannot tell you what I do not know. Some of this particular story concerns a preacher, but some of the chapters are about a great many different people, and surprisingly, even about you.

Either by your own choice or by someone's invitation, you are reading this book of stories. Some will be new to you, or they all may be. In a 24/7 society saturated with technology and multimedia alternatives to occupy our minds and time, a little book of stories might be a bit underwhelming. It certainly may not seem like an entertaining expenditure of your time, but resist the temptation to dismiss this book of stories. Go back to a simpler time, a slower time, and allow your mind to be drawn into stories from a book. Unplug and re-discover the written word. Take a risk and open your heart to the God who penned these stories. Find yourself in them. Allow one far greater than I to speak to you.

As you move from one chapter to the next, you will realize that God is a wonderful storyteller. You will also discover that we all have stories about how God works in our lives, and each one reveals how he speaks to us in any circumstance of life. As we turn the pages each day and move into the chapters, we need only open our eyes to see the wonder of our own special story. These stories vary in the telling of the details, but there are some constants within each: a person is there; God is there; and he looks for ways to speak to the person, often in unexpected ways. When the person hears God's voice and responds, the results are never ordinary, and something beautiful always happens. Perhaps by the time you turn to the last page, you will find something has changed within you. God has the power to use even a little book like this one to work wonders in anyone who will spend time with him.

Where is the middle of this story in which you now enter? Because it involves a preacher and God, you might expect to find yourself in places like churches or cathedrals, the places where we think God speaks. However, this story unfolds in undesirable places, sometimes in unsafe places, which are often frequented by the people who would never be found in cathedrals or church buildings. It is where the unexpected occurs quite frequently. To hear the story of this preacher, you have to be willing to go into the world of the neighborhood bar. Would it surprise you to hear the voice of God there?

Remember this though, the important question to answer is not, "Where does God speak?" The important question is, "When God speaks, will you hear?" Whether it is in a bar, in a church or in a book like this, will you hear?

"The wind blows wherever it pleases. You hear its sound, but you cannot tell where it comes from or where it is going. So it is with everyone born of the Spirit."
Jesus, John 3:8

Part 1

Chapter 1

What feelings arise within you when you hear the word *family?* We all know what the word means, but the meaning of family is different for each person. The family story of some people is filled with joy and treasured memories of shared loved while others are drawn into dark pits of pain every time they recall their family story. A simple but powerful word draws us down decidedly different paths.

A family may be less than what it could be, but a family can always be more than it is. The same is true of each individual since no one is completely limited by circumstances and situations. Into each life God speaks, and depending on whether we hear him or not, we have the possibility to rise above or fall below our possibilities. For better or worse, no individual is untouched by family experiences. Even though we are shaped by our families, an even greater force affects us more, a loving force. Those who hear the voice of God and listen, experience life far beyond the boundaries imposed by circumstances of family. These are the stories of God.

In this particular story, you will find that generational decisions in one family played a decisive role in the life of one young boy. The first characters you will meet on the pages of this story are his grandparents when they were young. This man and woman loved each other in simpler but darker times so do not expect a fairy-tale ending. As this story goes, the Great Depression and the Second World War were unfolding and these events made life difficult for this particular family. Scratching out a living sometimes meant long, hard hours of work on a dairy farm, living off the wild produce and creatures of the land, even uprooting the family to follow work. Through the years of their marriage, the man and woman were blessed with many children. They experienced the joy of the birth of a son, but they also knew the mixture of joy and sadness when twins were born next and only one survived, a little girl. As the years passed, three more sons and two more girls were born into this family.

This man and woman had met in church and often regularly attended that church. However, the man also went to bars on weekends where money much needed by the family went instead into the registers of those bars. Those were hard times to live through for everybody, and this family struggled to survive like so many others. When the preacher at their church was discovered having an affair, the effect on this family shook what faith the man had. This singular event would have a ripple effect on his family for generations to come. The father decided that he wanted no part of church if that was how preachers behaved, and he and his wife stopped going to it or any church except for an occasional visit. While a few children would go on their own for a while, the direction was set and even the few stopped.

With God removed firmly to the fringes of the family's life, they became more vulnerable. The father favored his sons over his daughters and showered them with more attention. He would carry the same attitude through much of his life even with his grandsons and granddaughters. Both sons and daughters, grandsons and granddaughters suffered from this uneven love, but in vastly different ways. If you have experienced either side of favoritism, you know all too well the damage such love brings to a child's heart and life. You know how such love can make a family more fragile.

It came to pass that when the father's sons were old enough he would meet them at the street corner near their house and take them to the local bar with him. For some young men this would make for a wonderful way to pass a Friday evening. For those sons, drinking at the bar with their father must have felt like a rite of passage into manhood. The father gave no serious thought about the effect such a practice would have on his family, at least none of consequence. Because he gave little thought to such things, he spent the bulk of his paycheck on liquor for himself and his sons; as a result, there was no money to buy food for his family. This forced his wife to step into the gap and enter the workforce. The man had no way of knowing then how Friday nights at the bar would shape his family, and he knew even less how God would use it to shape his oldest son and a future grandson. Even then, the man's story was not his own since God would have his hand in the writing.

Somewhere and somehow, the oldest son, who had been given his father's name, looked at his family story and wanted something different. He had known the joys and fun of boyhood as he played with his brothers, sisters and cousins. If he was not doing chores or farm work, he spent days catching snakes, dueling with wasps in a hog house, fishing or enjoying some other boyhood adventure. School filled many of his days for a while, but due to the times, his childhood was interrupted when he dropped out of school to help provide for the family. He grew up in a tough world and learned from his father the lifestyle of someone who goes to bars. Through all of this, or perhaps because of all of this, he longed for something better when he grew into a man. A restless discontent stirred within him. He wanted something different, but he did not fully know what "different" looked like, or even how to get it.

This young man's first step led him into the US Air Force where he set out for new places and a new start for his life. This decision led to rapid changes in the young man's life. The air force sent him far from his home and stationed him at a base in a town vastly different from any place he had known before. He traded lush, green rolling hills for dusty, dry, brown plains. Instead of the friendly faces of family, his days were now filled with the faces of strangers and fellow airmen. In this new environment, the young man had to make his own way in life, but his resolve held firm as he began to form a new future for himself. One day, something quite unplanned happened - he met a young woman. She was unlike any one woman he had known, and perhaps a far cry from the kind of woman he thought he would love. She intrigued him. A goodness resided in this woman that he had not experienced in his life. He did not fully understand this quality in the young woman because the source of it was God, and God had not been a part of his life for a very long time.

The young man was so affected by this woman that his interest grew into love. One day, in a simple ceremony, they pledged their lives to one another in marriage, and in this different place, far from his home, the young man started his own family. He soon would become the father in the story as his father became the grandfather. Within a year, he and his wife had their first child – a daughter. Within another year they had a son whom he named after himself. Yes, life had changed quickly for the new father. Unknown still to him, it had changed permanently in ways he could not imagine, and those changes would dramatically affect the life of his son.

Before their children arrived, the young man and his wife kept God on the fringes of their lives. He had no problem with this, but his wife struggled. When their first child was born, his wife decided that she had to put God back into the center of her life, and so every week she took up her daughter and walked to a church to worship her God. The father had absolutely no desire to go to that church or any church, but he would not stop his wife. Things became more complicated, however, after the birth of his son. Now when his wife wanted to go worship on a Sunday morning, she had to carry her one-year-old child and her newborn baby. This was considerably more difficult. Moved by compassion, a family at the church began to give the woman and her children a ride home in their car. This made at least part of the trip easier for the mother, but it also made it harder on the father. He began to feel like he was a bad man for not even offering his wife a ride to the church building in the first place.

Soon his sense of honor and duty compelled him to do just that, but he would do no more. Stubbornly refusing to go inside the building and worship God, he drove his wife and two children to the building and stayed in the parking lot in his car. This worked well for a while, but in the summertime it grew hot sitting in that car as the temperatures rose. While he sat in the car, sweating, the people inside the church building enjoyed cooler air. His resistance began to wilt in the heat, and the father decided it would be more comfortable to sit inside the building until the service was over. God had no problem using these circumstances to speak to the young man as this new chapter unfolded in his life.

While the father sat in that church building, he tried to mind his own business and still not worship. He was respectful and bothered no one as he sat there in silence; however, he could not help but hear. Eventually what he heard began to get through, and he heard more than a preacher preaching a sermon or people praying and singing hymns. The father finally listened to the God who was speaking to him. God had been calling to the father through his wife, through his children, through the summer heat, and now he spoke through those Christians. The day soon came when the father answered that call and gave his life to God.

You should consider that pledging one's life to God in baptism during a worship service is one thing, but being true to that pledge is something that affects more than one day. Such a life altering decision, if faithfully kept, leads to a new life that eventually conflicts with the ways of an old life. When this happens, such a decision will reveal itself to be either sincere or false. That time of revelation would soon come for this father. Painful pages had to be written and lived through as God penned more of this man's story. The man's new life could no longer peacefully co-exist with his old life, and a collision was headed his way that he could not avoid. This occurred not once or twice but every time the father took his family on vacation. He always took his family back to his parent's home where they would stay for a whole month. When they went on these vacations, he fell back into the ways of his old life. Fridays would come around, and he would meet his father and brothers at the street corner and head to the neighborhood bar. He wanted to spend time with his own father, and that meant going to the bar on Friday nights. Even though the young man had given his life to God, he found it difficult to break free from his old life for fear of hurting people who were dear to him. Perhaps you know this fear, and perhaps you find it written in other ways in the pages of your own story.

The inability of this young man to break free from the ways of his old life brought strife into his family. He and his wife argued over whether or not he should go to the bar every time their family went on vacation. Going home did not bring the joy it should have or could have; instead the experience brought stress, hurt, and pain into their marriage. Finally, everything came to a head and exploded on one fateful trip. The young man's son was five-years-old, and this little boy became a new voice for God in the man's life. As Friday afternoon came upon them, the father prepared to meet his brothers and his father at the street corner. When he headed out the door something happened that had never happened before – his son followed him out of the house, crying because he wanted to be with his father. The father now faced a dilemma he had not expected. He wanted to be with his own father, and that meant going to the bar; however, his son wanted to be with him, and that meant not going. Would he listen to his father or to his son? That is when his wife spoke: "You can go to the bar with your father and brothers if you want, but your son is getting older. One day he will want to go to the bar as well, and there will be no way that you can tell him no. You have to decide if you really want to go to the bar."

At that moment the young man heard. He heard more than just a troubled wife and a crying son. He heard the voice of God, a voice that finally reached this deep place in his heart. He decided then and there that he would not be the influence that would lead his son to drinking at the local bar. He turned around and did not go the bar with his father that day or any day after that. God spoke to him through a crying son and a godly wife. Because he listened not only did he stop going to the bar, but *his* father also stopped going as often. It turned out that his father wanted to be with him just as badly, and if his son was not coming to the bar to be with him, he would just go home on Fridays and play cards with his family. Unknown to a five-year-old boy, his life started down a different road on that Friday afternoon. His entire future was significantly shaped by his father's one simple decision to not join his father and brothers at the bar on Friday nights.

Take a moment and set this story aside. As you hear the telling of this one family's story, remember that it is a story that is not written just with human hands. God makes a way to have his say in every human story. The same is true with yours. He does not always communicate in an audible voice, or in dreams or visions. If you turn back the pages of your own story and reflect on your past, you will see the places where God has picked up his pen and written something for you. You only needed eyes to see or ears to hear. Looking back now, you may observe how he used a person or an event, sometimes enjoyable, sometimes painful, to re-direct your story. You did not notice him at the time, but God was involved with you so that he might bless you. Your story was being interwoven into a far greater story as God invited you to join him in writing something very special. Now – days, months, even years later – you decide what is written on the next page of your life. You decide if you will hear when God speaks into your story.

Chapter 2

It is time to pick up again the story of this young father and his family. As we move further in, our attention begins to turn towards the young boy. After his father's fateful decision, you might think that bars would no longer be part of his life. That would be a reasonable assumption, but you must remember that God wrote this story, and there are often unexpected twists in his stories. You know this to be true because you are aware of the twists in your own story. You also know some chapters of life are bittersweet. When we reminisce, we often hurt as the painful memories come flooding back as well. However, because God is involved in the writing, he touches our lives even in the bittersweet chapters. He speaks to us in all things, hoping we will hear him.

In every life, the sweet and the bitter entwine so closely that one is rarely far from the other. This would be true for the young boy as he moved more to the center of this story. His father's new way of life and the resulting differences became clearer as the years passed. Sweet times included vacations with family. The boy spent time with his grandfather and his uncles. They were fun men to be with, and he loved the experience. He watched them drink, laugh and enjoy one another's company whenever they were together. During one summer, he served as a batboy on their softball team, a team sponsored and named after the same neighborhood bar his grandfather and uncles still frequented. The boy enjoyed those times, but he did not long to follow in the footsteps of his grandfather and uncles. He steps were being directed by his father, a man who walked with God.

The years passed, and the boy's father retired from the Air Force. In the father's heart lay a deep desire to share with his own father and mother, as well as his brothers and sisters and their families, the special relationship that he had come to know with God. He wanted them to know the joy and the peace that had come his way as a result. He longed for them to see the genuine difference that had come about in his life because he listened to God and to see how his home had been blessed as a result. If God had done this in his life, he knew God would do the same for his family. He and his wife talked and prayed about this desire in their hearts, a desire that eventually guided them to move back to where the father's family lived. They would strive to be God's voice to family, but would anybody hear?

Initially, one of his nieces did as she joined them in worshipping God with a local church. This really was a wonderful and joyous event but not at all surprising to the niece. She had been raised by the patriarch and matriarch of this family, the grandfather and grandmother, and even though they had long since stopped being part of any church, she could recall walking on her own to a nearby church building to worship when she was five years old. She loved God and gladly heard his voice. Would others respond like her? Time would tell.

It was often difficult for the boy's father to be God's voice, because it seemed like his father and brothers did not believe he was really different. They did not understand how his heart had genuinely changed. They expected him to go back to his old life, but the boy's father would not waver from the ways of the God who spoke to him now. At every family gathering, through the routines of daily life, during times of family crisis, the boy's father used every opportunity to speak for God. His words and his actions spoke boldly in a multitude of ways. Having witnessed patriarchal favoritism as a child, he resolved to counteract it with love and attention when he saw his nieces being neglected by their fathers and grandfather. When his own father complained about how their involvement with a church was getting in the way, he stood up to him and refused to decrease their involvement with the church. At difficult times of testing, the young boy's father stood solid as a rock for his God.

The boy had become a teenager and as he went through his high school years, a desire burned strong within his own heart. When the day came for him to decide what to do with his life, he did not go the way of the bars, nor did he even enter the air force as his father had done. He walked in the *new* way his father had set before him. He walked towards God and set out for college. A young boy had become a teenager who then became a man, who would one day become a preacher.

He was not born a preacher; he chose to become one. His life as such took him down new roads and into new places. On the journey, God spoke to him in a multitude of ways – through people, through experiences, through his Word and through his Spirit. Sometimes, the young preacher knew it was God, but at other times, he was shaped by God in ways he did not recognize at the time. God began to pen new chapters in the young preacher's life that would prepare him for days when the unexpected would routinely come his way.

The young preacher often went back home to visit his family. He joined his father and mother as they all tried to speak to the whole family about God. He eventually would marry, and his own wife became part of the story. The young preacher was always amazed that his grandfather and his uncles, who had spent much of their time avoiding churches and going to bars, would look to him with deep respect just because he was a preacher. How ironic that the grandfather who had stopped listening to God because of a preacher now had one for a grandson! Those were times of sweetness, but the bitter trailed not far behind.

One day, the young preacher discovered that his grandfather had Alzheimer's. The disease did a cruel thing to his grandfather – it took his voice. Even though he could no longer speak, his grandfather remained completely aware of all his surroundings. The young preacher and his wife went home for a visit, and when they walked into his grandfather's house and said, "Hello," his grandfather began to cry. He broke down because he could not speak to his grandson. The young preacher's heart wrenched as he watched his grandfather weep. No more would he hear his grandfather's voice.

However, it would not be his grandfather's fate to die the slow death caused by Alzheimer's. A doctor diagnosed that he had advanced cancer, and not too long afterwards the young preacher received a call from his father bearing the sad news. His father asked his son if he would present the eulogy at the funeral whenever his grandfather died. That time came sooner than the young preacher expected because his grandfather died not long after his cancer diagnosis. Before his grandfather died, the young preacher's father had the opportunity to be God's voice one more time to his own father. On that day, the young preacher's grandfather heard. In fact, he had been listening for a long time, and before he died, he turned his heart back to God. At the funeral, the young preacher, along with another brother, spoke to the family. On that day, they spoke for God to all who were present. Did anybody hear?

Just a few years later, the sweet and the bitter would be companions of the young preacher once more. Almost four years after his grandfather's death, he and his wife rejoiced at the birth of their first daughter. With great joy his parents came to see their new grandchild. The young preacher's heart overflowed with joy as he watched his father and mother hold his daughter for the first time. When the holidays arrived, the young preacher took his wife and newborn daughter to celebrate with his whole family. The time was sweet and the memories made were precious. Then the bitter arrived, and impending death once again cast another dark shadow over the young preacher's life. This time the dark shadow of death was more intense because it was *his* father that was dying of cancer. This news devastated the young preacher and turned his world upside down. The two voices that had spoken for God so many years of his life were those of his father and mother. Now one voice would soon be silenced. Like it was for the young preacher's grandfather, so it was for his father, and death came too soon, just months after the diagnosis. The time for the father to speak to his family was drawing to a close. The young preacher's father had shown his family how a man of God lived; now he showed them how a man of God died. Through the way he faced death, his father courageously spoke for God one more time.

When the young preacher's father died, the whole family was enveloped in the suffocating shock. It seemed like they had been forced on a roller coaster ride they did not want to take. In the flurry of a few months, they had been turned upside down, twisted and plummeted down one drop after another. All they could do was hang on. Now the ride had ended and they had to get off – but without this special man of God. Numbness wrapped itself around all of them as they struggled to find a way forward. The young preacher's father had died, but he knew he would carry on what his father had started, alongside the rest of the family. His father's voice would not be silenced. As a family, they took up his mantle and spoke. The deafening pain of death would not silence their voices. God would speak through them. Would anybody hear? They prayed that one day the whole family would.

As it turned out, somebody did hear. Years of speaking for God began to show an affect. The young preacher's father had given many years of his life in this endeavor, and he and his family had made many sacrifices to do so. He died not seeing much come from those sacrifices, but God's voice had been heard. It was one of his brothers, as well as his wife. They too committed their lives to God and began to live for him. Unfortunately, they only listened for a short while. The brother could never break free from the bar and the drinking that had consumed his life. Just a few years after their baptisms, he and his wife divorced. One dark day the brokenness of a life lived too much at the bar came to a tragic end when the brother took his life. The sweet had become very bitter. As the shadow of death visited again, the preacher joined his mother and sister to speak again to the whole family about God. Because he was the preacher in the family, the young man was given the honor to speak at his uncle's funeral. He wondered if anyone would hear now.

Have you noticed that as you travel through the story of your life that death never stays away for very long? Death is one visitor we all wish did not know our address, but there is no place we can move on this earth where we cannot be found by death. The young preacher found he would have to taste the bitter again when death returned to his family. This time it was his grandmother, his father's mother, who died. She was a kind-hearted woman who had lived a long life serving all in her family. Many times the preacher had sat at her table and ate a meal his grandmother had prepared especially for him and his wife and children. When his grandmother died, the preacher joined his sister in speaking to the whole family about God, but it was no longer just them. At his grandmother's funeral other family members joined in and spoke up for God as well. God had been writing in their stories as well, and they had heard him. Many had listened when God spoke through the preacher's father and through their whole family.

Through these funerals, the preacher began to notice something – a family that had been known for going to bars was becoming a family known for going to God. Not all listened yet, but change was occurring. More bitterness would have to be tasted, and death would visit many times more before others would listen to God's voice; however, the presence of God was taking hold in more parts of the family. The family was becoming more than it had been, something different and something better. They were becoming a family that knew God better than they knew the bar. In the bitter, God had spoken and brought about something sweet.

This is how we come to the middle of the preacher's story. Now you know how a young boy became a preacher, a preacher who was familiar with people who go to bars. The bar would never be totally absent from his life, and he would one day find that the journey of a preacher would take him back there. Many fascinating chapters remained to be written. Each page turned would reveal another adventure in walking with God and speaking for him. In these pages, he would encounter people who would hear the voice of God as well as those who would not.

Now it is time to take a breather and reflect on your own story. Quite possibly some bar has played a pivotal role in your own life. If so, you know the reasons why. Pain, heartache and loneliness invades our lives in countless ways. Any void or emptiness in our lives will demand to be filled. Many people frequent bars not because it is their first choice, but because it addresses a deep need in some way. Maybe a bar has not been part of your life, but "bars" come in all shapes and sizes, like gyms, community organizations, internet sites, social media and even church buildings. God can be found and heard in any of these, but often he is found in too few of them. Too many stories are written without input from his loving divine voice, and lives are broken as they hurtle toward unhappy endings. Are the pages of your story tear-stained too often? Do you long for more of the sweet and less of the bitter? Perhaps as you read further, you will be able to hear God speak to you in the pages to come.

How, then, can they call on the one they have not believed in? And how can they believe in the one of whom they have not heard? And how can they hear without someone preaching to them? And how can they preach unless they are sent? As it is written, "How beautiful are the feet of those who bring good news!"
Romans 10:14-15

Chapter 3

The voice of God is never silenced. It has always been there since the beginning when God first spoke his creation into being, and it has been among people ever since. It cries out from generation to generation. When necessary, it skips a generation, but many times it is passed on from father to son or from mother to daughter. Because God speaks, one boy became a man, that man became a preacher, and the preacher began to speak for God.

He was not like the preachers he had come to know, nor was he like the ones he saw from a distance. He did not feel particularly wise or clever, nor was he bold or courageous. He felt nothing like what he thought a preacher should feel like.

"Who am I to speak for the voice of God?"

In truth, he just felt plain and ordinary, but perhaps the voice of God can be heard in the plain and ordinary at times when it cannot be heard otherwise. Perhaps the preacher did not have to be bold and courageous or particularly clever. Maybe he just had to follow the calling in his heart.

"Who can question God when he calls?"

So the preacher began a life of learning to listen for God's voice. Sometimes he seemed to hear him clearly; at other times he struggled to hear. Slowly a way to hear God began to come together for him. The preacher realized that each piece played a vital role in discerning God's voice. He had to spend time reading the Bible for insight into God's mind and will. He would need to humble himself more often in prayer and seek the one who was speaking to him. He would need to seek his wife's counsel as they both grew in the Lord. Finally, he would have to wait for his spirit to be at peace with any decision before he acted. Often the preacher struggled to do these things, but even when he failed, he realized that God never failed to help him get where he needed to be.

Through the years, the preacher learned to trust God to direct him from one place of ministry to another. Each time, his faith was stretched by every new door he walked through. He found that those who speak for God have to re-learn lessons about control. He had lived much of his life as if he was the one who controlled the events, but now he found himself relinquishing what little he actually had to follow the voice that directed him. His plans were often superseded by the unexpected. Sometimes tranquil waves gave way to stormy seas. Sometimes he had to step out in faith not knowing where firm footing would be found. To follow God's voice meant he had to embark on a journey of trust, something that can only be done one step at a time.

At this point of the preacher's story, life for him and his family had been good. They had known their share of struggles, but they were always blessed with enough food for their table and enough money to pay their bills. They had lived in one house and served in one church for eleven years. Many friends had graced their lives and home. Then it came to pass that the preacher felt God calling him to a new place. The whole family now had to face the challenges of a major move for the first time. The destination? A place the preacher had never desired to go. His own brother lived there with his family, and his brother had often spoke to him of coming to this place. For reasons that seemed valid to him, the preacher had always declined those offers. However, this time he could sense that God was closing the door on his work where he now lived, and the preacher knew he needed to allow God to speak through his brother's voice.

Following God to new places carries excitement as well as a fair bit of trepidation. The unknown is not for the faint of heart. The preacher would discover that his family's upcoming journey would prove more difficult than he could ever have imagined. If he had known what lay ahead, they may never had taken it. The bitter and the sweet would once again mix in the preacher's life but more intensely than he had ever experienced before. He would go through some of the most exciting experiences of his life, right alongside some of the most painful.

Journeys with God often turn out this way because God's primary enemy always seeks to prevent any effort to spread light into the darkness. This enemy would exact a price from the preacher and his family on this journey. A livable salary promised by good-hearted people would too quickly disappear. For a man with a wife and four young children, this would be no little turn of events. No weekly paycheck sometimes meant not knowing where money would come from to put even a single gallon of milk in the refrigerator or to pay the medical bills for a sick child. Peace and rest were often in short supply, and the strain weighed heavily on the preacher and his wife. On this journey through turbulent and uncharted waters, the preacher and his wife struggled to hear God's voice in the midst of the storms that whipped around their family. Following God's voice came at great cost for them.

If you take a moment to reflect, you may have wondered why your own life proved so painful at times. Whether you knew it at the time or not, you were not alone in your times of pain. You were in the presence of the enemy. He no more wants light to enter your life than he does anywhere else. You may have even heard God's voice and obediently followed, expecting that everything would go well for you. Perhaps you were surprised that even more trouble came your way at that point in time. In your own life, you learned the painful lessons that the preacher and his family learned. Though unseen, this common enemy is real in every life, and he exacts a terrible price from all who would follow the voice of God.

However, tough times and trials do not mean journeys with God should not be taken. When people follow the voice of God, they receive far greater blessings than any price exacted from them by the enemy. At such times, people truly learn to walk by faith and not by sight. They learn to raise their sights to higher vistas, they open their minds to new realities, and they give their hearts to greater dreams. They have done more than trade a life of ease for a life of uncertainty. They have swapped an unfulfilling life for a blessed life.

"Ahh...but we must get back to the story."

A major move brings excitement, and so it was for the preacher and his family. They looked forward to living near extended family for the first time ever. New friends, new opportunities, new adventures lay on the horizon for them all. Moving may have been a new experience for this family, but they eagerly rose to the challenge.

Shortly after he and his family relocated, the preacher began the challenging process of learning about the area and meeting the people in the community. He decided to walk through every neighborhood and leave a message on every door. As he did this, he would talk with anyone he encountered. He felt this was a good start for getting acquainted. On one memorable day, he walked through a neighborhood tucked around the corner and just a bit down the road from the little church building where he served. The young preacher hoped the people would hear the voice of God in the messages he left with them. Almost without noticing, he found himself walking by the open door of a bar on that morning.

"Surely no one there would be interested in what I am offering," he thought. He began to pass by, but God would not let him.

"Whoever is in there could use this message, too," a voice seemed to say to his heart.

The young preacher was certain that any efforts he made to speak for God in this bar would be rejected. He could use his time better by going to other doors. He actually preferred to go to those homes and pass by the bar and the people who drank there.

"Who would ever think that people who frequent a bar would want to hear the voice of God? Those people are only interested in drinking and drinking some more. They would rather give their money to a bartender for drink than to a grocer for food. They care not about the things of God. Such people would not even recognize God's voice if they heard it! After all, God speaks best and is heard best in churches and cathedrals. Can anyone hear his voice over the laughter of drinkers?"

Thoughts like this may be common among those who go to church buildings, but God often does the unexpected.

The preacher did not really understand what was happening. He only knew that sometimes God wanted him to do things that made no sense to him. He had promised God that he would walk through any door opened for him, and with that it was settled – the preacher listened to the stirring in his heart and went into the bar.

"Is the owner of the bar here?" he asked two women he encountered inside.

"I'm the owner," said a small woman on the far side of the bar.

That simple verbal exchange was the beginning of a relationship the preacher never anticipated. God would speak to him through this small woman and teach him many things in the years to come.

He soon found that God's voice could be heard very well in a bar. He learned that these people were not much different than the men he knew as a child. They had families. They had worries and concerns. They had hearts, hearts that could easily be touched by God if someone would be his voice, and so the preacher became that voice.

This particular bar was run by a small woman with a very big heart and great courage. How amazed she was when the preacher walked in that day. She was befuddled when he kept coming back. She was stunned when she learned that she could go to the little church building on the highway and be welcomed. In time this woman who ran the bar went to that small church with her grandchildren and a couple of friends. She began to hear God's voice and was overwhelmed. It was a voice that she had not listened to in a long time. She would come again and bring even more people from the bar with her.

When the preacher visited her at the bar, the small woman often would introduce everyone who came in for a drink to him. She had been talking to them about him, and most could not believe that a preacher would come into their bar and talk with them. They frequently were shocked to find themselves talking to a real live preacher as they drank their beer.

As this story of a preacher unfolded, God's voice was heard in the most unusual of places through a man who never imagined where his path would take him as a preacher. The story of redemption became the fare of that little bar. Such stories remain vital to us all because they are not just about God redeeming people who hear his voice in a bar. They remind us that redemption is offered to those who frequent churches, too. They show us how God even redeems a man who wants to be a preacher, and along the way, shows him what it really means to live as one. When you read what took place in and around this bar, pay close attention to the stirrings of your heart. Your story is just as important, and it may be no stretch to see yourself in the story of the preacher and the people he met. With God's help, you may even write your own story of redemption.

If you have any encouragement from being united with
Christ, if any comfort from his love, if any fellowship with
the Spirit, if any tenderness and compassion, then make
my joy complete by being like-minded, having the same love,
being one in spirit and purpose. Do nothing out of selfish
ambition or vain conceit, but in humility consider others
better than yourselves. Each of you should look not only
to your own interests, but also to the interests of others.
Your attitude should be the same as that of Christ Jesus:
Who, being in very nature God,
did not consider equality with God
something to be grasped,
but made himself nothing,
taking the very nature of a servant,
being made in human likeness.
And being found in appearance as a man,
he humbled himself
and became obedient to death —
even death on a cross!
Philippians 2:1-8

Chapter 4

What kind of people go to a bar almost every day? Perhaps people who go to a bar are just like people who go every day to a fitness club or a civic club. Maybe they are even very much like the type of people who go to churches. Would this be shocking to find out? How different are people after all?

Before you read about the people who went to this bar, ask yourself, "Don't people seek to fill the same basic needs?" The answer comes pretty easy, doesn't it? Don't people just want to go where somebody knows them? They want to be around people who know their names, who know their lives and who still accept them. Doesn't everyone seek to find some place to belong? They go to different places searching for such, and when they find it, a basic human need is fulfilled. When people find such a place, they stay until it no longer meets that need. Everybody needs to belong somewhere to someone.

This little bar in this particular town was a real place. It had its own smell, its own character. It had a homey feeling about it that was as tangible as the people who sat on its barstools. This bar was just as real as the people who walked through its doors, and those people were just as real as you and me. Each person had a story that the preacher came to learn and appreciate. Each person in that bar touched the preacher's life in ways he could not have envisioned.

For a season, their stories would intertwine with one another's as God began to write something very special. You took some time to know a little about the preacher's father and grandfather, now take a moment to know some of the people at the bar.

The woman who operated the bar was a widow with black hair and small of stature. She had three sons and two very precious grandchildren at the time. She may have been small in frame, but she carried a lot of influence in the lives of those who came to the bar. She had two sticks she would use to keep people in line when needed, one small and one big, but she could hold her own with people without using either stick. More than once the preacher would be thankful that he never was on the wrong end of this small woman's correction. This woman was more than someone who served drinks. She was a friend, someone to confide in, and someone who cared and who could be trusted. To several she was a second mother. She was the glue that held this social circle together, the same way mothers can hold a family together. She was the one who everybody else turned to for advice and direction.

A father and son often came into this bar. The father was a decent man with a wife and two grown sons. The oldest son, who seemed to have more tattoos than skin, was a frequent companion who followed in his father's footsteps. They both had a generous and giving spirit, but they also had heavy hearts as they carried burdens within them that were too much to place on any man. The bar was a place for them to unwind and momentarily get away from their worries.

Another special man also entered the story. He was like a brother to the small woman who operated the bar. The two would share concerns with each other and help shoulder one another's burdens. When he was diagnosed with cancer, not once, not twice, but three times, his "sister" was there for him. When his father and mother became ill, she was there. Whenever tragedy hit, she was there. He stopped in the bar more for the time with his "sister" than for the drink.

Then there was a young man who was rail-thin. He seemed to know how to find trouble. Once, the trouble put him behind bars. Sometimes he was angry, but deep down, he wanted to do right. He was not close to his own parents. This rail-thin man drank to hide the pain. The small woman who operated the bar was indeed like a mother to him, a mother he desperately needed. Like every good mother, she tried to set him straight when he messed up. She knew just the words to say to get his attention. This small woman was probably the reason this man was still alive.

There was a time when you could go into this bar and meet a big man. He was a good friend to the small woman. He was like an uncle to her sons and to her two grandchildren. The small woman who ran the bar could confide in him, and he, too, shared his troubles with her. He had his own grown children who had their struggles. For him, the bar was a place to clear his mind and renew his spirit.

The preacher met a family of three at that bar as well. The father was another big man, one who had been known for his temper. He could be particularly angry if somebody riled him when he had too much to drink. He had a wife and teen son. His wife often came to the bar to seek counsel or just pass time. The bar was her place to step out of her troubles for a while. The small woman who ran the bar was like family, so when they did not know how to deal with a teenage boy stretching his wings, they sent him to the bar, not for a drink, but for straightening out from his other "grandma". Their son was fiercely loyal to this small woman. He knew tough love, and he returned this love.

One of the most unusual people in the bar was an older man, small in frame. He was not unusual in a bad way, but in a rather unique way. He had served under General Patton in World War

II. When the war was over, he swore never to own a gun again, and this was a promise he never broke. Because he had no family in the area, he was all alone. The woman who operated the bar did what came natural to her – she and her husband adopted this gentle spirit of a man even though he was much older than both of them. He needed a mother and she had the room in her heart to love another son.

There was yet another man who frequented the bar, an older man who kept a lot to himself. He was a widow who missed his wife of many years. His heart grieved her, and he never went through a day without mourning her absence. She had been the perfect woman in his life. Now his most constant companion was a cat, but he would come over to the bar several times a week and spend time with his friends at the bar. He enjoyed their company.

This cast of people also included two brothers who had been hardened by life. Toughness marked their character and their spirit as well. One brother had become so hardened that he often proclaimed to all that he did not believe in God. He rented a small apartment from the woman, one of two apartments that sat next door to the bar.

The man who lived in the other apartment was a divorced man who loved country music and who played the guitar. He stopped in everyday at the bar when he got off from work. Once he became very sick and could not work for a long period of time. Because he could not work, he did not get paid; because he did not get paid, he could not pay his rent. However, the small woman who operated the bar also managed the apartments. She just forgot about the rent because she would not put her sick friend out on the street. Even more, she instructed the others to help him as well. In fact, whenever anyone needed help, the small woman who owned the bar would start up a fund, and everyone who came in would pitch in what they could to help out. This man would always be one of the first to contribute to the collection. He watched over the small woman, even looking after the bar and the people there when she could not.

It was not just men who came into this small woman's bar. This last man had been divorced from a woman who later married someone else. She had given birth to a son with her second husband. She would still come to the bar and spend time with her friends there. Things did not go well with her though. Her second husband was abusive and left her. On top of that, she developed multiple sclerosis and slowly her health started to fail her. Eventually she could not take care of her young son. One day her second husband tricked her into sending her son to be with him for the summer. He never sent her son back as long as he was alive. This frail woman needed help and she needed friends. She needed family, and she found them at the bar.

Among the women who came to the bar, there was an older woman. She had become like a mother to the small woman who ran the bar. She lived alone in her later years, after her disabled son had died. She would sit at the bar with the woman who was like a daughter to her, and they would talk and laugh. They would listen to each other and give advice to each other, depending upon who needed it most at that particular time.

This story includes an older couple as well. The woman had an amputated leg and was not well. The man had a kind heart, but he had lost his confidence and direction when he could not work and could no longer pay the bills. He never got used to that. Both would come to the bar to forget their troubles and to be in a place where they could have some sense of happiness.

There were others who would come into the bar. There were the regulars, there were those who would come less frequently and then there were those who would drop in for a time and then move on. The preacher would get the opportunity to meet almost all of them. They all had one thing in common – they wanted to belong. Many needed a family, and they saw each other as that family. As they began to meet the preacher and listen to him talk about God, they began to see family differently. They began to see that they did not have to just belong to this family in the bar. They began to see that God was calling them to be part of his family. They learned that even they were special to him.

Some would one day accept God's invitation to join his family. Others moved more slowly. The hardened brother who claimed he did not believe in God, would tolerate the preacher, but he would also later whisper to the small woman who ran the bar that he really did believe in God. Once the small church where the preacher served needed some wood to build crosses. This hardened man who claimed there was no God missed the opportunity to build those crosses; however, he made sure the preacher knew that the next time he would be the one to build the crosses.

The man who lived in the apartment next to him started to open his heart to God's call and to the preacher. Many times he would go back to his apartment in the evening and read his Bible. Several years later, when the preacher had to leave, he was there at a special gathering to say goodbye. He and the preacher had become family in just a short period of time.

The man who lived with a cat would hear God's voice speak to him in a very special way. One evening before Christmas, several people from the preacher's small church went to his house and sang Christmas carols to him. He stood out on the lawn in his dress coat soaking in every note with a smile that spread across his face. He would never forget that night and how those people loved him.

On another occasion, the preacher took several young girls from the church to see the woman with an amputated leg and her husband. They took along some food to help fill the refrigerator and the young girls used their voices to sing to this couple. The couple heard the voice of God in those girls' sweet, young voices. This woman who seemed to be nothing short of ornery went through an instant transformation. Her heart melted in front of those girls as she became as sweet as could be. She would start going to the small church on the highway right after that, along with her husband. They found great joy and comfort there. She could not go often because she was very sick, but the preacher and several others from the small church would go to visit her and her husband. When she was in hospice care, they became her family since neither had any family near enough to help. When a hurricane led many to evacuate, the preacher made sure she was taken care of since she could not leave. She died soon after the hurricane passed. According to her wishes, her husband held her funeral at the small church that had become her home.

The angry young man you met earlier in the story would one night meet the preacher outside the bar. He and the preacher would talk about matters that troubled his heart. This young man listened, and to him, the preacher made sense. After that, he was not so angry any more. He began to talk to others in the bar about things he was learning. Sometimes he would remind the people that they needed to listen to God.

The father and his son with tattoos would soon start going to the small church on the highway where the preacher would speak the words of God. The father's sisters who lived in a state far away were amazed that he was going to church. They never thought they would ever see that day. One day this father and his wife would have to sit in court and fight for custody of two granddaughters. The small woman who ran the bar and the preacher went and sat with them.

The young man with tattoos would open up his heart to many new people. Both he and his father loved to cook. They would cook for the people in the small church whenever they could. This young man with tattoos would find a special place in people's hearts as he offered his gift of cooking. With some great joy, he would try to see if he could make something too spicy for the preacher and would always be sure to invite the preacher to taste test his food as he watched on with laughter in his eyes.

In ways unplanned by the preacher but scripted by God, the voice of God was heard in one of the most unlikely of places by people who could never have imagined what was to unfold before their eyes. As a result, the family in this small bar changed as they heard God's voice. It grew in new and deeper ways as several became part of God's family, and as they began to accept people from the little church into their lives. This bar and the small church started to blend together as people discovered that both the church and the bar were places filled with people looking for a place to belong. This they had in common. As time passed, their faith in God would become even more common ground.

"I tell you the truth," Jesus replied, "no one who has left home or brothers or sisters or mother or father or children or fields for me and the gospel will fail to receive a hundred times as much in this present age (homes, brothers, sisters, mothers, children and fields – and with them, persecutions) and in the age to come, eternal life."
Mark 10:29-30

Chapter 5

Who speaks up for the poor?

There was a poor man who was one of those lost souls trying to find his way. He had no place of his own to rest his tired body. He was indeed poor. Even worse, he was poor in spirit. He had destroyed his life, and now his life was fading away. In his youth he had been reckless and angry, caring nothing for the law; he cared mostly about himself. Once he consumed too much alcohol and tried to drive home. This poor, drunk man hit someone while he was driving and killed that person. He was convicted of vehicular homicide and sentenced to prison. One night of drinking led to one life killed and one life flushed down the toilet.

When he was finally set free, this poor man set about reclaiming his life. Still angry and restless, he did not find success. His body turned on him before he had the opportunity. He had lung cancer. He was dying, and nothing could be done about it.

Who speaks out to the poor and sick?

This poor man's life was soon to turn around because his sister had been going to the bar operated by the small woman. She, too, had met the preacher and had begun to hear the voice of God speak to her heart. She began to go to the little church where the preacher spoke about God. Her heart was moved by what she heard and even more by what she felt.

This woman also began to speak for God though she did not know him well. She spoke to her brother. This angry, restless, young man listened to the voice now speaking to his heart. Should he be angry that his life was ebbing away? Should he curse his fortune and turn his back on the one who now called his name during his time of misery?

Is it not God who speaks to the poor and sick? Surely, he does, but will he speak out for the poor and sick when the poor and sick call out to him?

This poor man went to the little church on the highway when he was able and began to call out to God. Like the others from the bar, he wanted to hear the preacher speak for God. He wanted answers to his questions. The poor man and the preacher spent time together as they talked more. Time was running out though. Many times they were talking in a hospital room as the poor man struggled for breath with the little strength he had, strength that was slowly but surely ebbing away.

The poor man's body was getting weaker, but something remarkable was happening to his spirit. It was coming to life for perhaps the first time. His eyes were filled with excitement as he began to hear God speak to his heart. As his spirit began to long for more, his desire to be with God increased. When he was out of the hospital, he had to wrap himself up in warm clothes because his body was easily chilled, even in the warm spring air. Bundled up, he would go to the small church on Sundays to worship God and to hear his voice through the preacher's words.

On one of the Sundays after the preacher had finished speaking, he stood before the church and asked to be baptized into Jesus. God's voice was calling to him, and he was answering. Many tears were shed that day as this poor man became a child of God. He was no longer an ex-convict. He was no longer a former drunk, and he was no longer poor. He was a child of the King with all the rights and privileges of an heir.

Indeed it is God who calls out to the poor, but who speaks up for the poor?

This child of the King, though rich in the kingdom, was still in a body that was poor and rapidly fading away. Each day he grew weaker. Just a brief time after his baptism, he took one last trip on an Easter weekend. He went with his new brothers and sisters in the kingdom to another state for a weekend of joy and worship. It was a special trip for him as he soaked in the joy and wonder of young people as they praised God in many ways. He reveled in the new friendships of people who truly loved him. It was a marvelous weekend. Then the weekend drew to a close and, unknown to him, he returned home to die.

Death is no respecter of persons, but it can be unusually cruel to the poor. When that happens, someone needs to speak up for the poor.

On this dear brother's last day, the preacher got an unusually early call. His friend, this child of the King, had been living with his sister and her family in a run-down trailer. He had carried himself to the bathroom, and it was there that he died. His sister called the small woman who ran the bar who then went to them immediately. The small woman who ran the bar then called the preacher. He also went immediately to the family. He knew that was where God wanted him to be.

The sister and her husband had called the funeral home so that they would come and pick up this poor man's body. However, the poor man was indeed poor, as was the family. In fact, so were the small woman who ran the bar and the preacher. On top of all this, the poor man and his family did not have any insurance. Those who were at the funeral home knew that they would not be paid well for this poor man's funeral. Thus they were in no hurry to pick up his body. While they took their time, the poor man's body lay on the bathroom floor. Those from the funeral home would afford no dignity for the poor on that day. Thus the sister and her husband, the small woman who ran the bar and the preacher waited – for one hour, then another, then another and then some more. Who would treat a family this way just because they were poor? Who would leave a poor man's body lying in his own blood? Why would someone allow the body to stiffen and start to decompose just because the man was poor? Would they have hurried to the spot if this man had been rich?

Who speaks up for the poor?

When the men from the funeral home finally came to take the poor man's body, they did that and no more. They left the family the duty of cleaning up the blood and body tissue their brother had coughed up as he died. In anger the poor man's sister cried out. Her husband silently went about cleaning up the blood and human tissue from the bathroom floor. The small woman who ran the bar kept shaking her head and asking, "Who could treat a family like this at such a time?" Some days it does not feel good to be poor. On such days it seems as if no one with power speaks up for the poor.

On this particular day the preacher tried, but how does one man help a poor family confront injustice so that they do not become bitter? There is no man who can do this, but God can speak through a preacher with a humble and seeking heart to say what needs to be said to the poor at such times. On that day God helped the preacher speak to the hurting family.

However, the indignity this hurting family would experience was not over. When the sister went to the funeral home to make arrangements for her brother's service, she was to discover once more that she was poor. She was treated as if she was unimportant. She was hustled through the process of the arrangements, arrangements that were as convenient and as cheap for the funeral home as possible. Why should they lose money serving the poor? No one at the funeral home took the time to listen to this woman.

Afterwards, she went to the preacher, upset and troubled. She had wanted the service to be at the small church but was not given the choice. She had wanted something special, but no one at the funeral home was listening to her because she was poor. However, the preacher listened. What was done could not be undone, but his brother in the kingdom would have a memorial service befitting a child of the King.

On that day, the funeral chapel filled up with fellow brothers and sisters of the kingdom. They sat with the family and they cried with them. They sang beautiful songs and offered up heartfelt prayers for someone they loved, even if just for a short time. The preacher spoke the words that God had given him to speak. They were words of comfort and words of victory because this was not just a poor man that was having a funeral. The poor man who had been a drunken killer and an ex-convict, who had been an angry and reckless man trapped in poverty, was no more. A new creation, a child of the King had replaced him, and he was going home. He was going home not as a pauper but as an heir to claim his inheritance.

The funeral home may have thought they were just taking the body of a poor man into its doors, but it was the body of royalty that was laid to rest that day.

Who calls out to the poor?

Who speaks up for the poor?

Surely it is God. Because he does, they are no longer poor in his kingdom.

"Woman, where are they? Has no one condemned you?"
"No one, sir," said the woman caught in adultery.
"Then neither do I condemn you," Jesus declared.
"Go now and leave your life of sin."
John 8:10-11

Chapter 6

It has been so long that the dust had to be shaken off these memories to recall the man with no name. It is true! As you go deeper into this story in which you find yourself in the middle, there is a story about a man who had stopped using his name. He had walked away from his past and taken on a new life, a new name. How does a man live when he has no past? Can a man without a past have a future? Can a man completely throw off his identity and find a better man in its place?

The man with no name was in search of a new life. Actually, this was his third life, that is, his third attempt at a new life. His first wife had died, and thus ended his first life. He married a second wife and so began a tortured second life. She was as different from his first wife as a poisonous viper is from a dove. She was wild and unfaithful. Many times the man would come home to find her drunk, and sometimes her underwear had been soiled by another man. This hurt him deeply and angered him at the same time. The two began to quarrel. She accused him of striking her. His life and hers were going down the tubes. Finally, he could stand it no more and decided the marriage had to end.

As things had gone for his life in general, so went the proceedings for ending his marriage – terribly. He was living in his wife's town. She knew all the people; he knew none. He ended up on the streets, and she ended up in the house with all his possessions. He took whatever jobs he could to get by. He just wanted the proceedings finalized so he could go back to his old home in another state and start his life all over again.

The trouble was that this man with no name had lost his way. He started to hang out at different bars in the town. Eventually, he ended up at the bar run by the small woman, and somehow this bar seemed different. The people seemed like good friends. Many of them talked about a preacher and a little church around the corner on the highway. When the small woman asked him his name, he made one up. With no real name, he could be as lost as he wanted to be. He was lost in his nightmare and knew no way out. He was not even sure he wanted out.

One night, the man with no name came back to the bar. The small woman who ran the bar called the preacher and asked him to come and talk to this lost soul. The preacher came on over and sat down to talk with the man with no name. When this man trustingly shared his story with the preacher, the preacher shared with the man some words from God. The lost man began to listen. For the first time in many long, hard years, the man began to hear God speaking to him again.

On the next Sunday, this man with no name went with the others to the little church on the highway. It was a wonderful morning of worship that ended all too quickly. Before he left, the man talked to several other men in the small church on the highway about a job opportunity he had the next day. It was a physical job and he needed some tools, but he could afford none. One good man, a wise elder in that small church, offered to bring him some tools later that day. His experience in the small church that morning brought the man with no name renewed hope. For the first time in a long time, he was looking forward to the next day.

Once the time of worship was over, the man with no name had to go back to where he lived. His home was no more than a small room in the hotel. He hated to go back to his hotel room. It was not a good place. It was next door to another bar where bad things happened. He hated his room. It was a reminder of what his life had become, a life that he had come to hate. How could he have fallen so low?

The wise elder at the little church dropped by later that day and gave him some food and some tools so that he could go to work the next day at his new job. The man with no name received the gifts with deep gratitude. He was encouraged now that things were finally going good for him. His hope for a new life had been renewed by these good people at the small church on the highway.

However, when the devil has a hold on a person's life, he does not let go very easily. That night the man with no name found himself even more lost. He was about to go lower than he ever thought possible. On that dark night, he heard a knock on his door. It was the police. They had come to arrest him.

"What reason would they have for arresting him?" you may ask.

He had been charged with going to his former house and striking his wife during a heated argument. His wife was from that town, and she knew several officers. She had filed charges that day, and they were quick to take her side. For that reason, the man with no name ended up in a jail cell across the street from the little church on the highway.

When the preacher heard what happened, he went to visit this lost man in the jail. The man with no name told the preacher his story. He claimed that he had not hit his wife, she had lied, and he was being set up for a fall. The preacher was not sure whether or not he could believe this man because he barely knew him. However, he knew this man needed help. What did God want him to do? He did not know, so he prayed for guidance to the God who answers prayers and left it in his hands. He asked God to release this man from jail if he was truly innocent. If he would do that then the preacher would help the lost man all he could. In the meantime, the preacher would offer what little help he could while the man with no name sat in jail. He and the small woman who ran the bar prayed many times for this lost man in the days to come.

The preacher went to the man's hotel room and picked up the few things this man had. He took them and put them in storage in the attic of the church building. They would hold on to his meager possessions until everything was resolved. For the next few weeks, the preacher went across the street to the jail and visited the man with no name. This lost man was always kind and gracious to the preacher. The preacher kept praying for him, as did the small woman who owned the bar. As things turned out, God did not take long to answer their prayers. The lost man with no name was released. The charges had been dropped, and his divorce was settled soon after his release. The man with no name was free to go, but go where?

The first night of his release, the man with no name slept in a ditch. He had no money and no place to go. The next day, when the bar was open, he went to see the small woman who ran it. He feared that if he stayed in town even one more day the police would arrest him again. He believed his estranged wife would make up some other reason to have him arrested, and he believed the police in that town would be eager to comply with her desire. He asked the woman to call the preacher.

When the preacher received the call, he went immediately to the little bar around the corner. Seeing the man released and all charges dropped, he was now free to help without reservation. He called several men from the small church. They would accompany this man with no name and help him retrieve his belongings from his ex-wife's house. He had been given permission from his wife to do so, but the preacher wanted to make sure he did not go alone. They would watch over him every minute to prevent the possibility of any trouble.

In the meantime, this man needed a place to stay. If he stayed in a hotel, he was sure to get in trouble again, either by his doing or someone else's. For that reason the preacher invited the man to stay at his house that night. Not until later would the preacher learn that a police detective had called the small woman at the bar. He warned her that she should not help this lost man. He claimed the man was dangerous, and they were waiting for him to cause trouble. In fact, they wanted to know where he was. The small woman who ran the bar knew better, and she did not reveal where the man with no name could be found. The detective could not have guessed that the man with no name was sleeping that night at the preacher's house less than one hundred yards from the very jail the detective wanted to put him in. That night the small woman who ran the bar spent much of the night praying for the preacher, his family and this lost man.

The next day, the preacher fed the man with no name breakfast, and then several men from the little church on the highway came together to go with this man to get the rest of his possessions. The man's ex-wife lay in wait for him. She was ready to call the police at the slightest excuse. However, she had not planned on several men from the little church on the highway coming along.

The preacher and another man, his nephew, were the first to arrive. They waited on the side of the road across from the woman's house. The woman saw them and became visibly upset. She promptly called the police. She wanted them to arrest the preacher and his nephew. When the policeman arrived, the woman came out and started speaking to the officer, obviously agitated. She kept pointing to the preacher and his nephew as she talked.

The officer listened and then told the woman that no laws had been broken, and he could not arrest anyone or send them away.

When the man with no name showed up with the other men, they gathered all of his things as quickly as possible. The police officer stayed around to watch, ready to arrest somebody, but the preacher and the men from the church kept close to the man with no name so that he could get in no trouble. When everything had been loaded up, they left.

This man with no name left many of the things he owned at the bar for safekeeping. He could not take everything with him on the bus, and he needed to get on a bus that day. The small woman who owned the bar bought some of his things with the little money she could spare so that the man with no name would have enough money for a bus ticket. She knew that if he stayed in town he would risk getting arrested again, and she would do all she could to help him avoid that. When she looked at this man, she did not see a troublemaker or an evil man. She saw a man who was lost and who needed help finding his way.

The preacher made sure the man with no name got out of town that day without any trouble. The man was now free to start his new life. This man would later call the small woman who owned the bar and told her to keep the most valuable things he had left behind for herself. It was his way of paying her back for all her kindness.

When the preacher had first met this man, he was lost and would not use his own name. He did not know who he was any more. However, as he talked with the preacher, the small woman who owned the bar or the other Christians from the little church on the highway, he began to find himself again. He began to see a better purpose for his life. This purpose now included God. As he and the preacher got to know each other over those few stormy weeks, he stopped using the name he had made up and began to use his real name. Adversity and bad decisions had taken him down a road where he had lost himself. A loving touch and the words spoken for God in the darkest part of this adversity helped this lost man with no name find himself again.

The dust has now been wiped away from this memory so that you can see how God works in wondrous ways to help people who are totally lost. You can see that God calls out even to people that do not want to hear his voice. No one is so far away from God that they cannot hear his voice, and there is no place on earth so dark that his voice cannot penetrate the darkness and reach them.

"Suppose one of you has a hundred sheep and loses one of them. Does he not leave the ninety-nine in the open country and go after the lost sheep until he finds it? And when he finds it, he joyfully puts it on his shoulders and goes home. Then he calls his friends and neighbors together and says, 'Rejoice with me; I have found my lost sheep.' I tell you there will be more rejoicing in heaven over one sinner who repents than over ninety-nine righteous persons who do not need to repent."
Luke 15:4-7

Chapter 7

There was a time in the recent past when you could walk behind the bar and find a nice, well-tended garden in the back of the lot. It was worked, tended and meticulously cared for by a man who was well into his eighties. He was a small man with the spirit and gentle nature of a child. You met him earlier in the story, but you will be greatly blessed if you knew more of his story.

In his eighty plus years, this man had seen a lot of history. As mentioned earlier, he had lived through the Depression and fought in the Second World War. In that war, he made seven invasion landings in Europe and never received so much as a scratch from the enemy. This gentle man rode out numerous hurricanes in his life and helped clean up after they stormed through the area. For most of his adult life, he worked as a full-time welder, even into his eighties. This man with a gentle spirit could tell you story on top of story, the likes of which you have never heard.

One story involved his marriage to a woman who had two children already. They were married for a number of years, and he loved those children like they were his own. However, he and his wife did not live "happily ever after" because she died early. Then the two children he had loved as his own turned against him. They set out to get every penny they could of their mother's inheritance even if it meant leaving this gentle man penniless. He decided he did not need anything the two children needed so he turned it all over to them, even the house he had paid for and much of his savings. He just gave it all to the children who were adults by then. He simply felt that was the right thing to do.

No one knew of any living family this man had, but he did not worry. He had become a good friend with the small woman who ran the bar. She knew of all that had happened to this man. While her husband was living, they did something quite remarkable and gave this man with the gentle spirit a trailer to live in. If he could give up his house, they could give up their trailer. As you have already read, they went even further – they adopted this man with the gentle spirit even though he was many years older than them. They just felt he needed a family. He gladly became their son, and he began to refer to the small woman as his mother.

By the time the preacher walked into the life of those who frequented the bar, this man with the gentle spirit was already wary of churches. The last one he had been part of seemed only interested in his money. This left a sour taste in his mouth for religion so he swore he would never go back, and he never did. In fact, he did not have much interest in any church anymore. However, his mother had been telling him about the preacher from the small church on the highway. Something in what his mother told him sparked his interest, or at least his curiosity. He began to talk with the preacher himself, and he began to go to the small church. Once he started, he knew that was where he needed to be. He promised everyone, including the preacher, that he would never stop going to that small church.

As this man with the gentle spirit came to know more, he decided that he would make an important decision. He would accept Jesus as his Lord through his baptism. He was excited because he knew that many of the people from the bar planned to surprise the preacher on that day. Seven of them were going to be baptized on the same Sunday. They knew this would bring great joy to the preacher. This man was so innocent and childlike in his spirit that he brought his own towel in case the small church did not have enough. He was so eager to be baptized that he practically immersed himself without the preacher's help. This gentle man of almost eighty years was eager and ready to serve his God and Lord.

That began a wonderful time for this man with the gentle spirit and childlike faith. He took home every piece of paper the small church handed out. This included every article the preacher wrote in the church's weekly newsletter. He took them home and kept them neatly stacked. He read them over and over again.

When he turned eighty, his friends from the bar bought him his own Bible. He asked the preacher to write a note in it and sign it. He began again to read the Bible, and he began to recall the stories that his mother had taught him from childhood. Once more he heard God speak to his heart through this precious book. As this man with the gentle spirit read his new Bible, he discovered what had been lost to him years before. With each new discovery, he was eager to tell the preacher what he had learned. Things like: "All the really important words are in red because those are the ones Jesus said." What a precious heart this gentle man had.

This gentle man counted every book, every chapter and every verse in his Bible. He knew how many chapters and verses were in each book. He knew the exact location of the middle book, the middle chapter and the middle verse of the Bible. He had all his notes written down and made sure to show them to the preacher. This happened on more than one occasion, but the preacher did not mind. He loved this gentle man's childlike faith and spirit. Many times this gentle man fell asleep on his couch. His Bible would be lying on his chest, his arms would be folded over his Bible and a smile would be on his face. Sometimes friends walked in on him at such times and worried that he had died, but he was just happy and restful in the Lord, this man with the gentle spirit and childlike faith.

It would be just a few years that the preacher would be able to stay at the small church on the highway. Even when the preacher left, this man with the gentle spirit and childlike faith never stopped being part of that church. When he made a promise, he remained true to his word.

There have been many times that the preacher wished there were more people like the man with a gentle spirit. Too many have turned away from this precious book we call the Bible. They think it is too hard to understand, but the preacher and the man with the gentle spirit know better. Perhaps, you wish you could have such a spirit in you. Well, take heart because you can. Anyone with the faith of a child can open the Bible, read it and hear God's voice speaking. You might want to start with one of the gospels. In many versions of the Bible, the words of Jesus will be in red, and those are really important words.

"The angel of the Lord found Hagar near a spring
in the desert...and he said, "Hagar, servant of Sarai,
where have you come from and where are you going?"
"I'm running away from my mistress, Sarai," she answered.
"Then the angel of the Lord also said to her:
'You are now with child, and you will have a son.
You shall name him Ishmael, for the
Lord has heard your misery...
"She gave this name to the Lord who spoke to
her: "You are the God who sees me, for she said,
"I have now seen the One who sees me."
Genesis 16:7-13

Chapter 8

People can live within a hundred yards of each other and still be worlds apart. They may pass each other every day but never speak a word to one another. They know each other exists but never acknowledge each other's presence. Such is the reality caused by deep-seated racial division.

Down the road from the small bar and around a bend, as one heads towards the river, there is a neighborhood. It is an undesirable community, in the sense that many people in the town wish it were not there. Indeed, many of the people who live there wish they did not have to live there. It is the local projects. It is there that the poor people of color dwell. It is a neighborhood infested with crime and drugs. Many people die in those projects, and not all die of natural death.

One day the preacher walked into that neighborhood. Those in his church who had heard about his intent to journey into that neighborhood voiced their concern. They believed it was a dangerous place, and he should not go there, especially alone. If he in insisted on going into this community, he needed to make sure he had some protection, some weapon, just in case.

The preacher would not be deterred and ventured into that neighborhood one morning. He did go with some "protection" though – he went into the neighborhood praying. He knew God was with him, and he knew that God wanted him to go there just as he had wanted him to go into the bar. The preacher knew he did not go into that neighborhood alone.

In his hands he had letters that he had written to people who lived there. It was a simple letter with a simple invitation that said something of the sort:

> *"You may wonder what a white man is doing in your neighborhood. I have come to invite you to join me in prayer. I will be back on Saturday at a certain time. I will sit here for one hour outside the community center. If you would like to come out and meet me, I would like to meet you. If you come out, we can talk with one another and pray together."*

The preacher put this letter on every door in that community. Surely people were watching since most of them had no jobs and were probably at home. They must have wondered what a white man was doing in their community and what he was putting on their doors, but no one came out to get the letter while he was still in sight.

The preacher's brother and sister-in-law were intrigued by this. They were both excited and scared. They wanted to go with the preacher into this undesirable community, but their fears were not easily dismissed. They engaged in their own time of prayer, and eventually their faith helped them overcome their fears. They would join the preacher on that Saturday in the projects. When the day arrived that the preacher was to go into that neighborhood his brother had to work and could not go, but his wife still wanted to go. She went with her husband's blessings and prayers. On that Saturday morning the preacher and his sister-in-law took the first steps of an uncharted journey with God and with the people who lived in that undesirable neighborhood.

The preacher and his sister-in-law arrived as they said they would and pulled out some chairs. They sat down in the designated place to read their Bibles and pray. They were not sure how they would be received, nor did they know if anyone would join them. Would they spend the whole hour by themselves, reading and praying alone? Would anybody respond to the letter that the preacher had put on their doors? For a long time, it was just the two of them. Who can say how many eyes peered out from their windows behind drawn curtains as they tried to figure out what these two white people were doing in their neighborhood? The minutes ticked slowly by, and the hour was almost up. It seemed as if nobody would accept the invitation to meet.

Then a door opened up across the street that circled the neighborhood. A man and his wife slowly emerged from their rundown apartment and slowly worked their way over to the preacher and his sister-in-law. They looked as if they had not been awake too long. They wanted to meet these people who were brave enough to enter their world. They did not know that the preacher and his sister-in-law did not feel very brave.

This man and woman felt it was only right that if two strangers invited people from the neighborhood to join them in prayer that somebody from the neighborhood should take them up on the offer. Since no one else seemed to be willing to do so, they felt it was up to them. They sat down and began to talk to their guests. They began to share stories with each other, and soon this man and woman were telling of struggles with alcohol and drugs. They were two people with trusting hearts. On that Saturday morning, the four of them spent their first time praying together.

The next Saturday, the preacher and his brother and his sister-in-law went back. They sat together and prayed with that same man and his wife. This time they brought their adult daughters with them and even invited the three as guests into their home. It was a simple gesture on their part, but in that gesture they revealed that they were opening up their hearts to these three strangers who had entered their lives.

The next week the three returned along with the sister-in-law's mother. She had been convicted by what she had heard and through prayer she found her courage in the Lord to go into those projects. Two worlds that had long been separated by race, economics and behavior were now coming together. God was speaking to this family in the undesirable community, but he was also speaking to the preacher, his brother, his sister-in-law and her family. He would soon start speaking to the small church on the highway. It was clear to the preacher that God was working through them all to bridge a divide in people that should never have been there.

On one particular Saturday, the preacher, his brother and sister-in-law went into the neighborhood with a different purpose. They did not go and sit down in the usual place. Instead they walked around the neighborhood and knocked on doors and began to talk to more people. More people in the projects began to open up their eyes, even their homes to the preacher, his brother and his sister-in-law. Perhaps some were even trying to open up their hearts. The preacher, his brother and sister-in-law began to meet the children. They also met men and women who lived in that undesirable neighborhood who were just like them in many ways. They met a family that worked hard to make the community safer and better for all. In truth, this undesirable community was filled with many precious and desirable people.

At each of these visits, they tried to speak for God to the people. They tried to build relationships with the people they met. Then they tried to extend those relationships to the small church that met on the highway. They would go back to the small church and tell the people what was happening in the undesirable community, and the people in the church would listen. It was exciting as two worlds that were separated by years of bad history began to mesh. Into such events the voice of God speaks great things. However, two worlds that are vastly different do not come together easily.

The people who lived in the projects seemed eager to share in the experience, especially for their children. The man and woman and their adult daughters that the preacher and his sister-in-law had first met would bring their children to the small church and worship with them. Others from the community would send their children to visit the small church on the highway. The people in the undesirable community even invited the church to come and join them for a celebration in their neighborhood. It was an effort to make their community safer. The church gladly came. Later the church hosted a car wash for the precious children from the undesirable community so that they could get school supplies. They shared several experiences like this.

God was speaking loudly to everyone.

However racism, drugs and alcohol and old lifestyles do not let go of their hold without a fight. Those who lived in the neighborhood did not know how to break free, or perhaps they did not want to break free. The church did not know how to break free from its past of racism and soon tired of serving those in the undesirable community. The preacher was not sure what he was to do. Should he stay? Should he keep on trying? He and his brother and sister-in-law prayed for direction. What were they to do?

One day the preacher received a phone call from the first man he and his sister-in-law had met in the undesirable community. His wife was in the emergency room. She had overdosed on cocaine. The preacher, his brother and his sister-in-law went to the hospital. They tried to comfort the family and speak the words God would have them speak. They prayed with them. Soon word came that the woman had died. That was a day of darkness for the family and for the preacher, his brother and his sister-in-law. It was the same darkness that had hung over that undesirable community for long time.

Not long after his wife died, the man from the undesirable community decided he had to move. He took his daughters and grandchildren and moved to another state. For some reason the bridge that had been built between the small church on the highway and that neighborhood began to collapse. After a while, the preacher and his brother and his sister-in-law stopped going into the undesirable community. Did people stop listening? Should they have kept going? Or had the door shut? The preacher was haunted by these questions, but he had no answers.

Why do people stop listening to the voice of God when something so sweet is happening? Maybe you know the answer because you have done the same. Maybe we all feel stretched too far when we are given the opportunity by God to cross some bridges. For whatever reason, we often choose to stay on our side of the bridge, but there is still hope for us all. That hope comes from God because he will never stop calling us to him, and he will provide another opportunity to cross the terrifying bridges in our lives. One thing we must remember about God – there are no undesirable people to him. He loves us all.

"I tell you the truth, the man who does not enter the sheep pen by the gate, but climbs in by some other way, is a thief and a robber. The man who enters by the gate is the shepherd of his sheep. The watchman opens the gate for him, and the sheep listen to his voice. He calls his own sheep by name and leads them out. When he has brought out all his own, he goes on ahead of them, and his sheep follow him because they know his voice. But they will never follow a stranger; in fact, they will run away from him because they do not recognize a stranger's voice." Jesus used this figure of speech, but they did not understand what he was telling them. Therefore Jesus said again, "I tell you the truth, I am the gate for the sheep. All who ever came before me were thieves and robbers, but the sheep did not listen to them. I am the gate; whoever enters through me will be saved. He will come in and go out, and find pasture. The thief comes only to steal and kill and destroy; I have come that they may have life, and have it to the full.
John 10:1-10

Chapter 9

She was just a shadow, briefly there and then gone. The preacher could not recall exactly how she entered his life. Perhaps she just happened to call the small church on the highway as she worked her way through the phone book seeking help. Her story was a sad story, as they all are when people start calling churches listed in the back of phone books. Like the shadow that she was, her life had been lived in the darkness of sin.

The woman was a mother of three children. No father was present. There was no one to support her or to help her children. She had no family or friends to call on who could help her and not enough income to pay her long overdue bills. Her children did not have the clothes they needed, and they were all hungry. Her most pressing need was her rent payment. If she did not have six hundred dollars by the weekend, she and her children would be homeless. She had nowhere to turn so she called the churches. Eventually she worked her way to the phone number for the small church on the highway. She called and the preacher answered. She told the preacher at the small church of her need and begged for help. How many times had she pleaded and begged for help, only to be rejected by the very people who should have been eager to help her and her children? Could the preacher hear the voice of God in this woman's pleas?

The preacher faced a dilemma as he considered what God wanted him to do for this desperate woman. The small church on the highway did not have the money to meet this woman's pressing needs, and he barely had enough to provide for his own family. Would God somehow provide so that they could help this woman and her children? The preacher had learned that God often speaks without giving details of outcomes, so he stepped out in faith and did something. It was the middle of the day, and there was no one from the church that he could call for assistance. He and his wife went through their food stock and gathered what they could spare. They went through their children's closets and gathered the clothes that their children could do without. It was not much, but it was what they could think to do.

The preacher then went off to find this woman who had floated into his life like a vapor and who would disappear as quickly as a shadow on a cloudy day. After some difficulty, he found her house. To no surprise to him, it was a rundown shack that might have been condemned in a different community, but in this community it looked much like all the other houses. It was a poor community off in the country, easily overlooked and easily forgotten by all but those who lived there.

The shadow woman met the preacher at the door and gladly received him and the meager supplies he offered. She was indeed grateful, but he could tell there was disappointment in her eyes as she struggled with the knowledge that there would be no money coming for her rent. How could she raise six hundred dollars in just a couple of days?

The preacher spoke to her the words that he thought God would want him to speak. He offered her several suggestions of places she could call for financial help. She seemed to listen, but she was pre-occupied. The preacher noticed that she looked dressed to go out for the evening, and now it was late afternoon. Perhaps that was why her thoughts seemed to be elsewhere. Still she was polite and grateful and listened to the preacher, and they prayed together before he left. The preacher invited her to come and meet the people at the small church on the highway on Sunday and worship God with them. Perhaps they could find some way to help her. She was gracious in her reply and accepted.

The preacher left, not knowing how the weekend would unfold for this shadow woman who had drifted into his life. Would she find the rent money she needed? Would she really take him up on his invitation to come to the small church on Sunday? If she did, would the people of the small church help her? Surely they would since they had helped many others in whatever ways they could.

Sunday came and the preacher looked for the woman to come with her children, but she did not come. Indeed, she was like a shadow. Would he see her again? Were she and her children now homeless? What would become of them?

The preacher tried to call this woman of the shadows. He drove by to see if she was still there. All of his efforts were to no avail at first. Then he finally reached her by phone. He asked her the questions that haunted his mind. Were they all right? Yes. Were they still in the house? Yes. Was she able to get the six hundred dollars for rent? Hesitantly she said, "Yes." Wonderful! How did she get the money?

Silence.

Finally, she spoke to the preacher. She had sold herself over the weekend to some men to be able to get the rent money so she and her young children could stay in their home.

Silence.

What could the preacher say to this woman who had been like a shadow in his life for the past few days? How could he help her deal with the shame she was obviously feeling? He was so sorry for the decision this woman felt compelled to make. Did she really have to make that decision? Was that really her only option? Would not God have offered her a different way if she had listened to his voice?

This woman who was like a fleeting shadow was polite as the preacher said a few words to her, but she was about to vanish from his life. She had made her choice. She had chosen her road. She was there in the life of the preacher for just the briefest of times, and then she was gone.

Should the preacher have condemned this woman for her choice? Her despair had robbed her of hope, and she had chosen poorly, but she had chosen for her children. Perhaps she was not as troubled by her choice as the preacher thought. Maybe this was not the first time she had sold herself to other men, and maybe it was easy to continue in her old lifestyle. Perhaps she was just ashamed because she had to tell the preacher what she had done. Maybe she felt shame in being caught. Perhaps she just felt trapped in her life. As the preacher wrestled with these thoughts, he knew just one thing – his heart was broken for this shadow woman who believed she had no other choice.

What would God say to such a woman who had made such a choice? The answer is important to us, isn't it? We know that we have made poor choices in our own lives for which we carry our own shame. If only we had listened to God, our lives would have taken a different turn, but we didn't. Now we live with the scars and consequences. The burning question is not is there hope for this shadow woman, but is there hope for us?

So I find this law at work: When I want to do good,
evil is right there with me. For in my inner being I
delight in God's law; but I see another law at work in
the members of my body, waging war against the law
of my mind and making me a prisoner of the law of sin
at work within my members. What a wretched man I
am! Who will rescue me from this body of death?
Romans 7:21-24

Chapter 10

You might think him to be ordinary. Nothing about him suggested anything otherwise. Being old in years, he was well past his prime. He lived in a modest trailer in a small trailer park. Nothing about the man hinted of greatness. You could not be faulted if you considered this man to be nothing extraordinary. However, you would be wrong because what God sees in people as extraordinary is often passed over by people as just being ordinary. If you will spend a little time with this man you will see what God did, and perhaps you will understand what God could do in you. You must remember that none of us are ordinary and God does remarkable things if we listen to him when he speaks.

The preacher met this man on the same day he first met the small woman who operated the bar. As has been mentioned already, he lived in a small trailer park. This park sat just a couple of blocks north of the bar and just around the corner and south of the little church on the highway. So it was that before the preacher reached the bar that day, he came upon this trailer park and met this elderly man who seemed to be very ordinary. On this particular day, as you recall, the preacher was passing out letters to the community. He hoped these letters would speak for God to the people. As he walked through those neighborhoods, he prayed that some would listen.

When the preacher walked up to this man's trailer, the man had just gotten out of his car and opened the door of his trailer to enter. The preacher walked up to greet the man, and they talked for a little while. He was a gracious man and thanked the preacher for the letter. Then the preacher moved on as the man went inside his home. The preacher would meet the small woman at her bar just minutes later, but he would not forget this older man in the trailer.

After several days had passed, the preacher decided to go visit the man in the trailer again. The preacher knocked on the man's door several times without an answer. Surely the man was home because his little car was sitting in front of his trailer. The preacher knocked again. Soon the preacher heard a shuffling noise in the trailer and saw the doorknob slowly turned. Indeed the old man was home. The door opened and upon seeing the preacher, the man called out in a welcoming voice, "Come on in." The preacher stepped in, and when he did so, he entered more than just a trailer – he entered into the life of a man who would prove to be very extraordinary.

The preacher sat and talked with the man in the trailer, and he began to hear the man's story. This man had been retired from heavy duty construction for many years. He was now blind in one eye because of a cataract surgery that had gone bad. He had another cataract in his other eye, but his doctor had warned him to not have surgery to remove it. If he did, he would likely lose sight in that eye as well. As a result, the man learned to function with one eye that saw very poorly. The sunlight hurt his eye and this led to the man living in a trailer with all the blinds closed. Whenever he went outside, he made sure to wear the darkest sunglasses possible.

One of his neighbors was an elderly woman. She became a treasured friend for this older man. She too was nearly blind but in a different way. She loved to watch her television, but she could only see a small distance in front of her. When she watched television, she had to sit right in front of the screen with her face almost touching it in order to see the images on the television. Her eyesight was so poor that she could not even read her television guide to know what programs were on and when they were on. However, she could cook, and she loved to do so. You may wonder why that is important to this old man's story. This is important because the old man in the trailer did not like to cook. It turns out these two elderly people each had a gift they could offer the other. The woman who could not see well enough to read would cook meals for the man who did not like to cook. In return, even though he could only see poorly from one eye, he could still see better than the woman, so he would call her each day and read the television guide to her so she could watch her shows. What happened everyday then was not the blind leading the blind but the nearly blind helping the almost blind. What an extraordinary friendship these two had as they looked out for each other.

The preacher liked to visit the man in the trailer for many reasons. Every time, he would knock on the door, the man in the trailer would open his door, see the preacher and boisterously holler out, "Come on in here!" and the preacher would step inside. The man in the trailer would offer the preacher a root beer. He also gave him a napkin so that he could wipe the top clean. Every visit the preacher made started like this. Then they would sit in their normal chairs and talk. The preacher would sit in the chair by the door and the man in the trailer would sit in his recliner next to a lamp. The preacher often felt like he was in the presence of one of his grandfathers. The man in the trailer would talk about his past life, his current week and his grandchildren while the preacher gladly listened. This may seem like an ordinary conversation to you about a man who lived an ordinary life but be patient a little and learn more about this man.

Sometimes the man in the trailer would talk of his wife. She had experienced a massive stroke several years earlier but had survived it. While she was in the hospital recovering everything looked good. One late afternoon, this man went out briefly to a store to get something for his wife. They were making plans for her release. While he stepped out, his wife had another massive stroke that surprised everyone. She died while her husband was at the store. This deeply hurt the man from the trailer because he felt he should have been there when his wife died. He had loved her, and even now he lived with the painful memory of not being there and never having the opportunity to say goodbye.

As the preacher sat and listened, he could hear the love in the man's voice for his wife. That same affection was evident when the man talked of his granddaughter and grandson. He lit up with the biggest smile as he talked about their accomplishments. He loved his son and daughter-in-law, and he could not contain his pride in his grandchildren.

After just a few visits from the preacher, the man in the trailer decided he wanted to visit the small church on the highway. At first he was self-conscious about sitting in the church with his dark sunglasses on. The preacher assured him this was fine, and that set the man from the trailer at ease. He enjoyed worshipping at the small church on the highway. Every time he and the preacher sat down and talked in his trailer they talked about things of God. Because the man did not have very good vision he could not read a Bible for very long, so he would sit and listen as the preacher taught him about God. God was speaking to this gentle man, and the man was listening. Again these may seem like ordinary visits filled with ordinary conversations to you, but consider how often older people open their minds and hearts to learn something new, especially in spiritual matters. Indeed these visits were far from ordinary.

One day it was evident that the man in the trailer was troubled. The preacher asked him about this. What the preacher heard was incredibly joyful and heartbreaking at the same time. The man in the trailer had come to the decision that he wanted to give his life to God and be baptized, but he had a problem. He had grown up in a place and time when segregation was the practice, even the law. As he matured, he began to see that skin color really did not matter. However, in the little church on the highway there was an unmarried woman who lived with a man of different skin color. They had two children. For the old man in the trailer, his past was coming back up and running headlong into his present. He did not believe the woman should be living with a man she had not married, but he could not accept that a white woman could live with or be married to a black man. He did not like that her two sons were children of mixed race. He knew he should not have such ill feelings about this woman and her two sons, but he found he could not easily break from his past. In the world he had known since his childhood, people of these two different skin colors did not inter-marry. The man in the trailer knew that until he resolved this, he could not be baptized. He knew if he were to claim Jesus as his Lord, he would have to love all people no matter what their lifestyle choices were. Carrying this heavy baggage from his past, this seemingly ordinary man faced an extraordinarily difficult decision. Would he, in his later years, hang on to the ways of his past, or would he embrace a future the Lord called him to that would take him in the opposite direction of his youth and heritage?

The preacher listened to the man in the trailer agonize over his struggle, and he knew that he would have to allow time for God to undo decades of segregation in this man's mind. He continued to visit and pray with this man. When he was alone in his office, the preacher often lifted up in prayer the man in the trailer. If the old man had to fight the racial demons of his past, the preacher knew he should stand in his corner through prayer.

One day the preacher went to visit the old man in the trailer again. He knocked on the door and the door soon opened. "Come on in here!" the man in the trailer said with a big grin on his face. The preacher stepped in, and the man in the trailer offered him a root beer and a napkin so that he could wipe the top clean. They sat down and began to visit. Then the man in the trailer said to the preacher, "I am ready. I want to be baptized." The preacher smiled as he heard these words. Then he asked the man in the trailer, "How do you feel about this white woman who has two sons by a black man?" The man in the trailer said that was no longer a problem for him. He had come to peace with that situation and with his past. Now he was ready to give his life to his Lord Jesus. Extraordinary!

The preacher and the man in the trailer went over to the little church on the highway that very day. On that day the man from the trailer entered into the kingdom and became a child of God. He could only see out of one eye, but he could see a whole lot better in a greater way. On that day the preacher and the extraordinary man from the trailer rejoiced with the angels in heaven.

It was just a couple of years later that the preacher and his family would have to move away. There were many difficult goodbyes for the preacher. One of the toughest was saying goodbye to that extraordinary man in the trailer. It would be the last time they would see each other. Less than a year later, the preacher returned to the area to bring supplies to the people in that small town who had suffered through a terrible hurricane. The preacher looked forward to seeing his friends again – the small woman who owned the bar, the little man with a childlike faith and the extraordinary man in the trailer as well. Just days before his return, the preacher received a call from his brother. The man in the trailer had died.

The preacher would not be able to see his dear friend again, but the funeral for this precious man would take place when the preacher would be in the town. He was thankful that the family gave him the privilege to give the eulogy for his dear friend. The funeral was held in that little church on the highway where an extraordinary man turned his back on his racist path and embraced the way of love that his Lord called him to.

One day the preacher and the man from the trailer will meet again in a better place where both will be able to see. On that day, Jesus will return and call the man from the trailer home. Jesus will look into the two good eyes of that good man and say to him, "Come on in here!" And like always, the extraordinary man from the trailer will listen to his Lord.

"You are all sons of God through faith in Christ Jesus, for all of you who were baptized into Christ have clothed yourselves with Christ. There is neither Jew nor Greek, slave nor free, male nor female, for you are all one in Christ Jesus. If you belong to Christ, then you are Abraham's seed, and heirs according to the promise."
Galatians 3:26-29

Chapter 11

Who determines where God proclaims his message? Does he only speak in churches? Who does God use to be his voice to the people? Is it always the preacher in the nice suit? Is it always the people with beautiful and nice lives that he uses to be his voice, or does he go beyond such people to use those with ragged lives to speak for him?

What if God chose to use a different means for his purposes so that people who never went to a church could hear his voice? What if he chose to do something that not only was unheard of by Christians but even unthinkable so that new people could hear him? What if he decided to use someone who ran a bar to proclaim his message? Could he do that? *Would* he do that? Would God use a small woman who runs a small bar in a small town to do his work and to be his voice?

Listen to what the preacher learned as he watched God do something special that does not happen every day. After all, what preacher would normally walk into a bar to be God's voice? Even more so, what owner of a bar would welcome a preacher? Is this not evidence enough that God would do such a thing?

Why would this woman tell everyone who came into her bar to buy a drink that she was talking with a preacher who dropped by? If he happened to be sitting at her bar, why would she tell whoever walked in to go talk to the preacher while she served them a beer? Was this not God working? Does not God sometimes work in ways that are mysteries to us?

In the preacher's story, weeks turned into months, which turned into years. The preacher would stop in at the bar frequently to talk with the small woman and those who had become his friends. He tried to speak to each one, as God would use him. Often the people would be sitting at the bar with their beers discussing what the preacher had said and what he meant. A change began to take place as attitudes and behaviors started to change. One was just as likely to walk into the bar in the midst of a spiritual discussion as any other topic. When someone would have some problem that the small woman who ran the bar could not solve, she would tell that person to talk with the preacher. Truly God was speaking to the people who frequented this bar.

How often had the good people of the churches wished that this bar, as well as other bars, were no longer in existence? There was one time when a tornado came down the street, tearing down houses around that bar, but strangely it skipped over the bar. Did the good people in those churches understand why this bar was spared? How many had thought that God had missed His target? What was he doing?

As time passed, the small woman who ran the bar began to understand the voice that spoke to her of wonderful things. This God was great and powerful; he was compassionate and full of mercy and forgiveness. What she had received at her baptism, she freely told others about. The voice of God became strong in her.

All too soon, the day arrived when the preacher had to leave the company of that little church on the highway. He would no longer be there to speak for God. His friends at the bar wondered what would happen to them. How could this happen? But God's plans are not always the plans of preachers. His ways are not always the ways of people who sit in bars. Sometimes God works in mysterious ways, and he only reveals it a little bit at a time.

When the preacher moved away, God took care of his children at the bar by bringing them another man to speak for him. It was the preacher's friend from a town nearby. This friend was also a preacher, a man of similar spirit who had no trouble going into a bar. The people in the bar grew to love this man, and he loved them as well. Then God brought the people in the bar another man to be his voice. This man was the preacher's brother. They had known the preacher's brother for as long as they had known the preacher, and the people in the bar loved and respected him. When God brought this man to them, it was like welcoming a long lost family member back home.

As God was doing all of this, he was calling these people at the bar to take up his call and be his voice. Some of them heard. None were yet very strong of voice, but they began to find their voice and began to speak for God. None spoke more powerfully than the small woman who ran the bar.

When a hurricane bore down on her town, instead of fleeing as many did, she hurried about looking after older people who could not get away. She scrounged what supplies she could get for them so that they could ride out the storm and its aftermath. When the storm had passed, she traveled about in her failing car to check on those people who could not fend for themselves. This small woman cradled an aged black woman in her arms as she died while others ridiculed her for caring about an old woman from the projects. She welcomed aid from the preacher in the nearby town whenever he would bring her supplies. Her bar became a distribution center for the poor who were often overlooked. The preacher from the nearby town would bring her supplies that she would load up in her car, and the small woman would take them to another city as she sought out strangers who needed those supplies. When she gave them those needed supplies, she shared with them a message from God. Often on these trips, she would have to call for aid from one of her sons because her car would break down in some unknown place.

How does one explain why one small woman who ran a bar would take on such a burden for the old, weak and helpless when many churches simply looked out for their own? How does one explain such a changed life? This is not something witnessed every day. Who is really the preacher? Is it the person who stands in hallowed halls every Sunday and preaches to the comfortable? Or is it the small woman who operates a bar and uses her place to speak for God to those with ragged, broken lives? Who do people flock to hear? Who did God send? Surely God uses both for his purposes. We accept one. Can we accept the other? Does God use all bars in such a way for his purposes? Unfortunately, it is not possible in every bar, but he could do similar things in every bar where people would listen to his voice.

In some bars, the voice of God is heard and answered. Those who hear the voice then take up the call and carry the message to others who have not heard. It is amazing that the voice of God spoken by someone in a bar sounds very much like the voice spoken by someone in a hallowed church. His voice is constant no matter where it is heard, so let us not be quick to judge people. If a small woman in a small bar in a small town can become a powerful voice for God then we have yet to discover all the places where his voice is being heard and who is speaking for him. Perhaps God's light shines best in such places at certain times. Perhaps those who speak for God in the churches could learn from those who speak for him in the bars.

Yet, as it is in churches, it can be in bars. You know this to be true – the voice of God can call out, but not everyone will hear. Some will hear only noise. Others will hear the voice clearly enough, but being in love with other things, they will close their ears and their hearts. When God's voice speaks clearly and the truth is undeniable, one can choose to hear and obey or choose to shut that voice out. Too many hearts shut him out and miss the wonder and power of the one who calls them.

The voice of God calls out, but who will listen?

"Here I am! I stand at the door and knock. If anyone hears my voice and opens the door, I will come in and eat with him, and he with me."
Revelation 3:20

Interlude

Now you know some of the preacher's story. You have met people whose life stories intertwined with his for a time. As I have already mentioned, I cannot share with you the end of the story for it has not been written yet. The pages continue to turn, and new chapters still remain to be written.

As you read the preacher's story, perhaps you remembered parts of your own. Yours is no less important, or any less remarkable, if God helps you write it. How is he speaking to you? How has he involved you in the plot? What wondrous ending does he hold out for you to discover? Remember this, you are in the story that God is writing because you are important to him. You are not just a minor character, but one of countless major characters. In your story, you are key because it cannot be written without you.

Will your story end well? If it were up to God alone, it most certainly would, but then your part would not be all that important, and your character would diminish. Sadly, not all stories end well because not every character listens for God. However, if you will look around you, it will not be hard to find others whose life stories are obviously being blessed by God. There are too many such stories to count. You won't necessarily recognize them by the abundance of money or the lack of trouble in their lives, but you will recognize them easily. Draw strength from them; allow God to help you write something special in your own life.

It might help you to know that God has been writing stories for a long time. He knows how to write them. In these stories, we can lose ourselves, and then find ourselves in ways we never imagined. There is one ancient story that God wrote that has been read by countless people. It is the best story he ever wrote. I share portions of that story with you now, neither the beginning nor the end – just more of the middle. Perhaps you will find yourself in the chapters of this most special story.

"In the past God spoke to our forefathers through
the prophets at many times and in various ways,
but in these last days he has spoken to us by a son..."
Hebrews 1:1-2

Part 2

Chapter 12

Who can say what childhood dreams this little girl had as she grew? Like every little girl, she had big dreams. From her childhood, she had heard great things about God. She had heard great stories about when this God had spoken to other people in ancient times. Perhaps she dreamed of a time when he would speak to her like he spoke to them. Would that not be a wonderful dream to have come true? Perhaps one day she would hear the voice of God speaking to her.

When do childhood dreams fall by the wayside? When do children give up their dreams and exchange them for the reality of their lives? Is not life cruel as it steals away one childhood dream after another? This little girl would grow into a woman and live among a people that were hated and despised. This woman and her people were used to being treated as trash. They received that hate and returned it in full force. Because of the hatred, there was strength in her people that came naturally to her. She could care less what people thought of her. While others looked down on her, she held onto a belief that she was good. She, just like her people, would be a survivor. Her dreams would become her reality and her life would turn out good.

There was one special dream this woman had as a child; it was the dream of every little girl as they grow into womanhood. She dreamed of falling in love and marrying the most wonderful man in the world. She and her true love would marry, have children and live "happily ever after." This was every little girl's dream, and it was her dream.

One day that special day came. It was the day of her marriage. It was the day that her special dream was to become reality. Perhaps her dream started out that way, but it was not a happily ever after marriage. It ended too soon for reasons that no one now knows. It left her with a broken heart and a wounded spirit.

Were her dreams of "happily ever after" cast aside? Not hardly. She was a survivor. Surely this good God would give her another chance at love. That opportunity did come, and then it too ended. Then there was another marriage, which ended, and another one, and another one… This tragic woman's story became shrouded in darkness. Her dreams had been shattered by life. Something terrible was wrong with her. She surely must be cursed. The God she had dreamed about as a girl seemed distant and silent. Could he not hear her cries to him? Perhaps it was true that she was trash. Why would the God of the universe care about someone like her? Why would he listen when she prayed? Why did she ever think that he might one day speak to her? The little girl with dreams had grown up into a disillusioned, lonely woman.

This lonely woman needed to be loved, but there was no one to love her. How would she survive? She settled for someone who would just let her live with him. He did not care enough about her to marry her. He did not love her. To him, she was just a slave, a servant. She did not like this, but at least she was off the street. She had a place to sleep and food to eat, if not a place to be loved, but then what good is love when you are hungry and alone?

She no longer dreamed. Women like her could not afford to dream. Though the dream may be sweet, one always has to wake up to reality. When dreams are crushed by reality, the pain becomes too much to bear. No, dreams were not for her.

One day she woke up and went through her day as usual. It was a day that held out no particular promise of being anything other than hard and long. One chore she hated was the drawing of water. When you live among a poor people, you walk to a well to draw water. It was a long walk to the well, but it would be even longer on the way back under the weight of the water she would carry on her shoulders.

As she walked to the well, she passed a group of strangers, a dozen men. She knew who they were, or rather, from where they came. They were people from the other country, the country that despised her people, and so they despised her, too. They did not speak to her nor did she speak to them, but she could see the hatred and spite in their eyes. How dare they look at her in such a way in her hometown!

She had almost forgotten about them when she came to the well. To her shock, and disgust, there was another man sitting at the well.

"Another man from that other country! Where did all these enemies come from on the same day? What was going on?"

She determined to just keep to herself. She would draw her water in silence and then head back home. That is what she would do.

"What was that?"

This stranger said something to her. Surely not. Men from his country don't talk to women from her country. But he did speak, and he spoke again. What did he want? Was she safe? Should she just drop her water jar and run away? No, she could not do that.

He spoke to her *again*! What did he want? He wanted her to give him some water. Was he crazy! Why should she? Who did he think he was! He kept speaking to her, and she could not be silent. Quite unexpectedly, she was drawn into talking to this man.

"Please, let him be quiet so that I can go home and do my chores for the man who does not love me," she thought.

Now *he* was offering *her* something. What! Now he was offering to get her some water. Why would he do that? How *would* he do that? He was a stranger passing by, and he had nothing to draw water with from this deep well.

He did not make any sense. Not only did he offer to get her some water, he offered her some special kind of water. Was he delusional? How could he say that whoever drank his water would never get thirsty? Perhaps he had escaped from some asylum. Surely he was crazy, but he did not look crazy. He did not act crazy. In fact, if he were not from this other people, she might be willing to talk to him.

Was he ever persistent! He kept on trying to get her to talk. Why did she even bother to talk back? Why couldn't he just leave her alone? Why couldn't he just let her draw her water and go home and do her chores for the man who did not love her? Wasn't her life bad enough?

"What did he just ask? He wants to meet my husband."

Who was he to make such a request of her? She would not stand his interfering in her life. Why did he have to ask her a question that caused pain to rise up within her heart? All she wanted to do was draw water and go home and do chores for a man who did not love her. Oh, how her day had turned into one of agonizing pain. How did this all come about so suddenly? Who was this stranger?

She did not want to talk to him anymore, so she just quickly said under her breath that she was not married. After all, it was the truth. She owed this stranger no explanation about the painful details of her life. She certainly was not going to share her shattered dreams with a stranger!

"You are right that you have no husband. In fact, you have had five husbands and the man you live with now does not even love you enough to be your husband."

Had she heard right? What did he just say? How could this stranger know her story? She did not know him. He did not know her. She searched his face looking for some sign of familiarity. Perhaps they had met once long ago or met in passing recently. No, he was not familiar. How did he know these things about her? She never talked to anyone about these things. They were too painful. Who was this man?

"I am the one you have been waiting for. I am the one who speaks for God."

Did she hear right? She had heard stories about the one who would come to her people and speak for God. Her people had longed for that day but had long since given up any real hope of this person ever coming. And if he did come, why would he speak to her? Was this really that man? How else could he know these things about her?

Everything was a jumble in her mind. She no longer knew what to say. Suddenly those twelve men that had passed by her earlier showed up. They were with this man. They looked like the kind of men who would travel with the man who spoke for God though she was not really sure what such men would look like. This must be the man who would speak for God! It could be no other! God was speaking to her!

She did not know what to do. What should she do? The only thing she could think to do was run. Run back to town and tell everyone who was at the well. Immediately she left her water jar and ran. She ran into town screaming for everyone to come. The people in town would surely think she was crazy. After all, why would they listen to her, a woman who had been married five times and now lived with a man who did not love her? Who was she to tell them anything? Why would they believe that God would speak to her?

The townspeople heard her screams. They were not sure what she said at first, and then they weren't sure about what they heard. What was this woman babbling about?

"The man who speaks for God is at our well!"

This was impossible, but someone was out there. Someone had gotten this woman all excited. They decided to investigate which meant there was only one thing to do – they all went out to the well.

Who was really at the well? Would he still be there? Yes, he was still there. They started talking with this man. Yes! It was indeed the man who talked for God. In fact, it was the Son of God! They never dreamed that God would come to them, a despised people, but he did! Not only did he come to them, he stayed with them for several days. It was a wonderful two days they spent with this one who spoke for God. Oh, those people of the other country who despised them would surely be surprised when they heard about this! What joy! But the greatest joy was in the heart of the lonely woman who had had five husbands and who was now living with a man who did not love her. Her childhood dream had come true. Who would have ever thought that God would really speak to her? All this time she had thought he did not care. She did not know that he loved her. Indeed, he had loved her more than she ever dreamed was possible.

(This biblical story is found in John 4.)

In the fifteenth year of the reign of Tiberius Caesar — when Pontius Pilate was governor of Judea, Herod tetrarch of Galilee, his brother Philip tetrarch of Iturea and Traconitis, and Lysanias tetrarch of Abilene — during the high priesthood of Annas and Caiaphas, the word of God came to John son of Zechariah in the desert. He went into all the country around the Jordan, preaching a baptism of repentance for the forgiveness of sins. As is written in the book of the words of Isaiah the prophet: "A voice of one calling in the desert,

'Prepare the way for the Lord,
make straight paths for him.
Every valley shall be filled in,
every mountain and hill made low.
The crooked roads shall become straight,
the rough ways smooth.
And all mankind will see God's salvation.'"
Luke 3:1-6

Is it possible that even today the one who spoke for God to a woman who felt unworthy and unloved is still speaking to the same kind of people today? Does his message still ring out, longing to be heard by lonely and broken people? Yes. He is still being heard. Maybe some tragic events in your life have caused you to wonder if God really loves you. Maybe you have gone through your whole life so far feeling like no one loved you. Think about this – you still have a future and you can go through the rest of your life knowing that you are indeed loved by a Father who loves all people, no matter what they have done or what has happened to them. You, too, are loved by this great God. Listen to him, he is calling to you.

Chapter 13

He could not remember his old life really. So much had happened. So much time had passed. How much time he could not say. He did not keep track of time anymore. Time was his enemy; it tormented him. In truth, he had too much time. He wished that he would have no more. He wished that he was dead.

Time is not the friend of one whose life had gone horribly wrong. How did it go so wrong? When did it all start to go bad?

"No! Don't think about it! Don't remember!"

The truth was he could remember, but it hurt so much he did not want to. It was too late. The memories were flooding in, and he could not stop them now. He could see the faces of his family. There were his mom and dad. Oh, how he longed to be with them. They always had the answers to his questions. They were always there to help him when he was in trouble. He always knew they would love him.

Then he could hear the laughter of his children. What sweet, precious children! The tears streamed down his face as he looked into their eyes and saw their love for him. There were never any more beautiful children in the world. He would roll with laughter whenever they played. They were always his source of joy.

Then he smelled the sweet smell of his wife's bread baking. Mmmm! How intoxicating that smell was! When was the last time he had tasted something so delicious? His memory wandered from the bread to the beautiful face of his wife. She had been the only woman he had ever loved. When they married on that day, he thought his life couldn't get any better.

The man did not know how right he was. His life had become a living nightmare. He did not even know why it happened, or how it happened.

"Why me? Why did they pick me?"

He had done nothing to deserve this. He didn't want them in his life, but there were too many of them. They were too strong, and they overpowered him. They turned him into a monster!

He could remember the look of horror on his wife's face. He saw the sheer terror in his children's eyes. Oh, how he hurt as he recalled their shrieks when they ran away from him! What had he done to deserve this? It was not his fault.

"I am not a monster!"

Then he opened his eyes and looked at himself. He looked around at his surroundings. He was naked! What decent man ran around without clothes to cover his body? His body was covered with scar tissue. His appearance was hideous. Around him was the smell of death. The smell came from his own stinking body that had not been washed since well before he cared to remember. The smell also came from his surroundings. He did not live in a house, or even in a shack. He lived in a graveyard! How did he end up so messed up?

"Ahhh! I am a monster!"

Everyone feared him. No one came near him. They had tried to lock him up because they thought he was dangerous. Was he? Had he ever hurt anyone? Would he hurt anyone? At one time in his life he knew he never would. He was a good man, but then *they* came and ruined his life. *They* helped him break free of his chains, not that he wanted to be free. He wanted to die! *They* were the ones who drove him out and forced him to live in a graveyard. *They* were the ones who tormented him so much that he beat himself and cut himself with rocks. His screams terrorized the countryside as they were carried by the night winds. No one dared come near him.

It was not always the same. Sometimes they left him alone to recall his old life, just like now. It was a fiendish torture, allowing him to remember. When they had their fill of that sport then they would do something else to demonize his body. He could hear them inside his head talking about him, telling him what they were going to do next. Then they would do it, and there was nothing that he could do to stop them. There were too many of them, and they were too strong.

"Why me? What have I done to deserve this? Why don't they just kill me and be done with it?"

He knew the answer to his question before he even thought it. They would not release him from his torment. They would keep him alive as long as possible while they tortured his body and soul. And when he could take no more, he would die and they would move on. Where would they go then? Whose life would they ruin next? How many times had they threatened to attack one of his children next? It must not be! He would hang on for them. Perhaps this was now the sad, twisted purpose for his life.

"Oh, no!"

They were getting excited. He could hear their voices again. What were they going to do to him now? They were screaming at him.

"Get down and hide!"

Why? What was happening? They sounded afraid. Afraid? Yes! *They* were afraid, but why?

"Get down and hide!" they screamed at him as they forced his body to the ground. They did not want to be seen.

They were talking about someone in excited but muffled tones. Who were they talking about? What did they call him? They paid no attention to this tormented man now as they cowered in fear.

The tormented man began to wonder, "Who was this who could make *them* cower in fear?"

He looked around and tried to peer through the darkness of the night. Down the hill something was moving. It was a boat. It slipped up to the shore, and some men got out. Those who had tormented him for so long became agitated. They were talking about one of the men. They hated him, but they also feared him. They knew him. They called him by name. Who was this man they feared?

"Wait! If they were afraid of this man, could not this man help me?"

Surely he could, but would he? It was worth a try. If only he could get to this man, but how? His tormentors would not allow it. They were too strong for him, but he had to try. This was his only chance.

"Run! Quickly! Don't stop! Don't let them stop you!"

His tormentors were taken by surprise. They had not expected this. What was the tormented man doing? He was running down the hill towards their enemy. They must stop him.

"Stop him or be destroyed by the enemy. Stop him!"

He fought his tormentors. He ran screaming down the hill, struggling for every step.

"No! Don't let them pull you back!"

It hurt too much to go on, but he must go on. This was his only chance. If he could just win this one time! All he had to do was get to this man they feared.

"Keep running! Keep walking! Keep crawling! Don't stop!"

Finally, he was there. In agonizing pain and exhaustion, he threw himself at the man's feet. He could not speak. He wanted to. He wanted to cry out, "Please help me! Give me back my life!"

He tried to speak. He started to speak, but it was not his voice. It was theirs! What were they saying? They were begging for mercy. They were not worried about him anymore; they were worried about themselves.

What did they call him? What was his name? Jesus? Who was Jesus? Son of the Most High God! That's who this man was. Could it be? Would this Son of the Most High God help him?

Then the tormented man heard the voice for the first time. It was the voice of the One who spoke for God, and it set him free. Could it be? Where were his tormentors? They were in flight, screaming as they rushed into a herd of pigs. Two thousand pigs then rushed down the hillside and plunged into the sea. Demons screaming, pigs squealing – it was awful! The chaos was deafening as the herd thundered down the hill. Then it was silent as each and every pig drowned. *They* were gone and gone for good.

Now there were more tears, but these were not tears of agony; he was crying tears of sheer celebration. He had been given back his life. He wept uncontrollably at the feet of the one who had saved him.

Then the one who spoke for God spoke to him. The man opened his eyes and looked into the eyes of the one who spoke for God and saw *his* tears of joy. The Son of the Most High God was crying for him. What kind of God was this? Somehow the one who spoke for God knew what he had been through.

As the man looked, he noticed that he was different. No longer was he naked. He was wearing clothes again! Where did those come from? He could not help but laugh at the sight. The sight? He looked and his scars were gone. Completely vanished! He no longer reeked of death either. Everything was new! Could this be?

Then the one who spoke for God asked him to sit down, and they began to talk. This was the greatest miracle of all, talking with the Son of God. What wonderful things he heard from the one who spoke for God. He could sit there all night and listen.

"What's that noise? What was happening now?"

People were coming, people from the surrounding towns. They seemed terrified. Why? They were afraid of the one who spoke for God. How could that be? Don't they know who he is and what he had just done? They did not know, but they were talking nervously to the one who spoke for God. Now he was leaving along with the men who had come with him!

"What! No, wait! You can't go! If you go, let me go with you. Please, let me go."

"No, you stay here and tell your people what God has done for you. Go tell them your story so they will know who I am."

"Tell my story? To my people? Yes! That is what I will do. Who shall I tell first? My family! My mom and dad! My wife and children! Run, quickly! Don't stop! Hurry home!"

(This biblical story is found in Mark 5 and Luke 8.)

"The Spirit of the Lord is on me,
Because he has anointed me
to preach good news to the poor.
He has sent me to proclaim freedom for the prisoners
And recovery of sight for the blind,
To release the oppressed,
To proclaim the year of the Lord's favor."
Luke 4:18-19

At what point do people realize that life's problems are bigger than themselves? We do not have to be possessed by thousands of demons to be enslaved to the same enemy. Who will recognize the one who speaks for God even when they are enveloped in darkness? Who will run to him in order to find deliverance? Each step will have to be fought for, but only by fighting to get to Jesus will one find deliverance. Only when we recognize our enslavement and run to Jesus will we be set free.

Chapter 14

Who can understand the bondage that position places on a person except those who know those chains personally? People who hold no position are not bound by the expectations that come with the position. They are free to do as they think, free to do as they please. They do not have to answer to the masses. It is the one of position, the one who leads the crowd that has to meet the greater expectations of the crowd. Heavy are those restraints on a man's heart, but heavier still are the chains placed on those who lead alongside other leaders. Perhaps this man is to be most pitied of all, for not only must he please the masses, he must also conform to his peers.

The freethinker should not serve alongside those who only seek to conform. That is a terrible strain that one places on self, desiring to be free but also desiring to be accepted. Such people often live in contradiction within themselves because they are not free to express what their spirit knows to be true when that truth is different from the accepted beliefs. One must either break free from the conformers, or one must put to death his spirit because no man can live peacefully while he is in contradiction with himself.

Long had this one man desired to be a leader. He had worked hard for his heart's desire. Many hours he listened to wiser men instruct him in the finer points of being a leader. Even more hours were spent in becoming part of their world. He knew how to pay a compliment to those he wanted to please. He knew when to speak and when to be silent. He knew the honor code of his society. He had become skilled in the fine art of politics. He knew that survival in such a world depended upon honing those skills well.

It was not that long until his time of recognition came. He became part of the ruling council for his people, and he became of one their leaders. He sat in council with the wise men of his society. Though younger, he could hold his own with the older men. He just had to know when to speak and when to be quiet. He had to know which way the winds blew before he made his thoughts known. Was that not the exercise of wisdom? He could go far with such an attitude.

Yet, a disturbance came into his tranquil life for which he had not prepared. Something unexpected occurred that no one could have envisioned. The man who claimed to speak for God intruded into his mind. Truly, that was his art. This man who spoke for God seemed to insert himself into the public mind at will. Indeed those on the council spent much time discussing him and keeping tabs on his activities.

Many on the council had gone to hear the man who claimed to speak for God. They came back with incredible stories. Sometimes they spoke of miracles that he had done. Those on the council were amazed at what they saw, but they would never say so publicly because as they listened to this man who claimed to speak for God, they discovered that they did not like him. He spoke harshly of those on the council. He told the people that those who were leading them needed to repent.

"Unheard of! No one speaks of the council that way and gets away with it. No, he is not a good man; he is an enemy, this man who claims to speak for God."

Being a member of this elite council, this young man listened to the talk that took place behind closed doors. He wondered what was so terribly bad about what this new teacher was saying. As he listened to those who served with him, he understood that they could not prove the new teacher wrong. However, new teachings never sit well with those who conform – especially when they feel threatened by those teachings.

This young man was on the same council, but he was not a conformer at heart. He had tried to be, but when he heard the words of the one who claimed to speak for God, he felt drawn to him. He liked what he heard, even if he did not understand it fully.

"Why shouldn't this new teacher be heard? Were not others free to move about with their teachings? Many teachers walk about and teach what they believe, and many times they disagree with one another. Many serve on this council and argue and bicker over finer points of the law. Why should this new teacher not be allowed the same freedom?"

These thoughts he would have to keep to himself when he was among those on the council because they would turn on him if they knew what he was thinking.

As this freethinking young leader considered the new teacher's words, he could not escape his appeal. He could not get his words out of his head. It was then that he decided to go and hear the man who claimed to speak for God for himself. He would go and talk with him directly and form his own opinion. He would not allow others to tell him what to think.

Pursuing freedom and a new direction is exciting and can be an intoxicating experience, but breaking free of conformity can be a dangerous thing for a leader. One must go about it with some measure of wisdom and caution, and so it came to be that this freethinker went to see the new teacher at nighttime. No one else on the council need know of his intent. He found out where the Teacher stayed and stole away at night to talk with him.

Words cannot express how his spirit was stirred that night. The words the Teacher spoke made his head swim with thoughts he had never considered. Surely this man did speak for God. He taught as no one he had ever heard before in all his years of training. There was authority in how he spoke and in what he spoke. He was like a fresh wind in a room that had long since grown stale and suffocating with dead air.

He stayed as long as he dared stay with the Teacher. He had to leave before he was discovered, but he now knew the truth. His mind raced with new thoughts and new understandings. In another place and another time, he would surely have followed this Teacher, but now he was a ruler on the council. He lived in a world where he had to conform if he wanted to survive. Being on the council, he had already heard some of the whispers of what they wanted to do to the man who claimed to speak for God. That was not a fate he wanted to share. Besides his people back home had their expectations of him that he must fulfill.

This is how the young freethinker started to live in contradiction with himself. He sat with men who hated the man he admired most. He sat in meetings with men making stuffy talks and meaningless points over trivial matters while out in the countryside the Teacher shared words from God that re-shaped people's lives. He would give anything to trade places with any of those poor who were free to follow the Teacher, but he had to live within the restraints of his world.

A man cannot live in contradiction to himself for long before the contradiction begins to torment him and the truth begins to leak out. Sooner or later that man has to make a decision. Either he will follow the way he believes to be true, or he will sentence himself to a tortured life of conformity.

One day as he sat among those on the council, he listened to their discussion about the man who claimed to speak for God. These men he used to admire and flatter looked different to him now. They were full of venom. They hated the Teacher and were infuriated by him. It seemed all they could talk about was how to stop him.

"What is so bad about what the Teacher tells the crowds of people who swarm to him?"

One day this young man almost made a fateful mistake when those on the council were ranting and raving about the teacher. The truth leaked out – a little. He forgot the rule of being silent when you disagree with the conformers if they are in greater number. While the men on the council were attacking the one who claimed to speak for God, he spoke up for him, offering up a point of law that he thought would be harmless yet helpful.

"Does our law condemn someone without first hearing from him?"

Quickly all eyes turned to him and turned on him. "Are you one of his, too?"

It was an instant and quick rebuke. He was startled at how quickly it happened. He had been careless. Would that be the end of it, or would they press him with questions? Did anybody detect how deep his true feelings went? Would they be suspicious of him now? He must watch himself because such outbursts can lead to worse things than a sharp rebuke.

The strain of the contradiction within him was increasing. The pressure was building, and he felt as if he would explode. Sooner or later, he had to decide who he would be. Would he conform against all that he now believed, or would he pay the price to break free from those who pressed conformity on others? That day rapidly approached, and this freethinker knew it. He knew the plans the council had to seize the man who claimed to speak for God. They would railroad him through a mockery of a trial. The Teacher he had come to believe in would be killed in a cruel and horrific manner. His voice would be silenced by those with whom he sat on the council. This young man had to make a choice.

The day came when these dark events unfolded before his very eyes. The Teacher was indeed arrested and eventually killed. It is said that the free thinking young man joined another man who also sat on the council, a fellow freethinker. He, too, had followed the one who spoke for God in secret. When the Teacher was killed that man went to the governor and claimed the body. Then gave up his own burial place for the Teacher to be laid. This young, freethinking man joined him in burying the one who spoke for God. It was a very public thing to do for one who served with conformers. Perhaps that is when he made his choice.

(This biblical story is found in John 3, 7 and 19.)

"If anyone would come after me, he must deny himself and take up his cross and follow me. For whoever wants to save his life will lose it, but whoever loses his life for me will find it. What good will it be for a man if he gains the whole world, yet forfeits his soul? Or what can a man exchange for his soul?"
Matthew 16:24-26

It is hard for God to break through the voices of those who seem to be concerned about our best interests. When people want us to succeed, when they want us to advance and even fight for us, we eagerly and faithfully listen to them. The closer those people are to our hearts, the harder it is to break free from them. Yet, what if they are wrong and what they want for us is not what is truly good for us? What if truth lies elsewhere? If God calls us down a different road, breaking free will bring sacrifice and suffering. Will we listen when God speaks to us then?

Chapter 15

It is no sin to be sick – in some places. In other places, if you are sick, it's just as bad as sinning. No one blames the sick for being sick in those places, but still the sick are cut off. No one else wants to catch the sickness. No one else wants to be contaminated. No one else wants to be unclean. Sometimes in such societies, compassion turns to pity, and pity eventually turns into disdain and judgment.

What if an important person were stricken with a long-term illness? How would the people react? What if it was a wealthy person or a popular and famous person? People might be genuinely concerned for their wellbeing. Probably many would feign interest, hoping to receive some kind of notice. However, if the sick person was a "nobody", someone insignificant, the response from society would be totally different. That person would be invisible to all except a few. In societies where people are consumed with their own advancement or survival, who would care for such a person very long?

In one such society, a certain woman had a particularly disgusting sickness – she was a bleeder. Bleeding is not a good sickness to have because blood can be terribly hard to disguise. It soaks through clothes and quickly becomes evident. Bloodstains do not come out, and blood has an odor that is readily discernible and very unpleasant to smell. In some societies, blood makes one unclean so that they cannot go to places of worship. Even coming into contact with blood can make one unclean. In such societies, no one wants to get around a woman who is a bleeder.

"Stay away from her! Ignore her. She is unclean, besides she is no one of importance."

It was like this woman was invisible to the masses of people who passed her by.

No one knew why this woman was bleeding, and because no one knew why, no one knew how to stop the bleeding. This invisible woman did not want to be sick. She did not like the feeling of being sick. She did not like feeling weak and dizzy due to the loss of blood. The woman had long been trapped in a body that had betrayed her. She had been sick for so long, twelve years, that she had forgotten what it felt like to be healthy. Abnormal had become normal for her.

This invisible woman had tried to find healing during those years. People would tell her about doctors who could help her, or the latest treatment that might work on her. She would go to those doctors and undergo their treatments. Sometimes they were excruciating; sometimes the treatment felt worse than the disease. She wanted healing so bad that she was willing to try anything, yet nothing ever worked. When she heard of some new possibility, her hopes would rise again.

"Maybe, this will be the cure!"

Always her hopes were dashed against the hard rocks of reality when the treatment was done. Those were the worst days – dejected, depressed and still a bleeder.

At some point do you give up hope? If you give up hope, you die. Those who want to live never give up hope. They keep trying and keep searching. It is their only option. The life of this invisible woman had been swallowed up in this dark and depressing realm of existence between hope and hopelessness.

It seemed this invisible woman had exhausted all possibilities of healing. Her body was weak and beaten down. How much more could she take? Even if she heard of some new drug or some new treatment, it would take time for her to gather enough money because those treatments were never cheap. Even when they did not work, she did not get her money back. Recently though her hope had been renewed. It did not rest in more doctors or more treatments but in someone different. Circumstances had changed. The man who went around the countryside speaking for God was also a healer. She had heard stories of him healing others, and she had met people who said they personally knew someone who had been healed. She had reason to hope again; this was the one she would go to.

However, there was one obstacle that blocked her hope – the man who spoke for God never seemed to come to places where she was. He traveled everywhere. How could she ever catch up to him? If she heard about him being one place, he would be gone by the time she got there in her weakened condition. She could not go ahead of him for who knew where he was going next? Still he was in the area, so she patiently waited for her time to come. She could muster enough hope to hang on a little longer.

One day her time did come, very unexpectedly. The man who spoke for God had been traveling nearby when a community leader had sent for him. The leader asked him to come heal his daughter. His daughter was dying, and he loved her so much. He could not bear the thought of losing his daughter who was so young and so precious to him and his wife. He sought out a healer, the one who spoke for God. When the community leader requested his help, the man who spoke for God consented to go with him. They were on their way to heal the little girl when word came that the girl had died. There would be no need to bother the Healer anymore. How the community leader's heart broke. His journey to the man who spoke for God had been in vain. The Healer did not stop though; he just proceeded on with a sense of purpose.

It was then that this invisible woman's time came. She knew the Healer would pass nearby, and she could see the crowds coming her way. She knew it was the man who spoke for God because nobody else drew such crowds in the area. As the crowds came by, she eased her way into the crowd so as to not draw attention to herself. She dare not try to stop the man who spoke for God. She would simply get close to him and touch just a small part of his clothes. Surely that would be enough to heal her.

The invisible woman had to be careful, for if anybody in the crowd recognized her, she would surely be cast aside and her one chance would be gone. She could not go on living if that happened knowing she had been so close to the Healer. Carefully, the woman worked her way through the crowd. It was not easy since the people were moving fairly quickly, and so many people crowded around the Healer. When you have been weakened by twelve years of bleeding, it is not easy to withstand the pushing and jostling of a crowd.

The woman tried to keep her eyes on the Healer, but he was up ahead, and sometimes people in the crowd would step in front of her and block her view. She struggled to regain her view and to gain ground on the Healer. She just had to get near him. She would bother him just for a touch.

"Please, let that be enough! Please let me get to the Healer! Help me, God, to reach him! Give me strength!"

Yes! She was getting closer. She could see a clear path to him now. Oh, if only no one would cut her off. If he would only slow down some, she could catch up to him. She was not sure she had the strength to go much further. She was closer now. Closer. She was there! She only had to reach out…

She reached and touched just the smallest part of his clothes. Would it be enough? Yes! It was! She could tell immediately. She had been healed! She *finally* had been healed!

"Praise God!"

Suddenly the Healer stopped.

"Oh no!"

"Who touched me?" he demanded to know.

"Who touched you? There are people all around you, everybody's touching you. What do you mean who touched you?"

"No, someone touched me in a different way because I felt power go out from me to that person. Who was it?"

Everyone looked about for the troublemaker. If the man who spoke for God said someone touched him then someone touched him.

"Okay, who touched him? Speak up so we can get on down the road to more important things. We have a dead girl to go see."

"I did," said the invisible woman as she meekly stepped forward.

She said it almost apologetically. Would the Healer take back the miracle since she had not asked to touch him? Would he be so cruel as to do something like that? She knew she was not as important as the community leader's little girl; she was just an invisible woman who needed help. She could not even pay the healer for his cure.

The Healer looked at her, but he was not angry. She saw him smile. Instead of an angry rebuke, he offered her love and a blessing. Then the man who spoke for God said to her, "Your faith has healed you. Go and be free from your suffering."

At that point this woman, no longer invisible, came to understand and know that no one is invisible to God. He sees and he cares. He looks for invisible people, hoping they will believe in him. He sees them. He hears them. Will they see him? Will they hear him when he speaks to them?

(This biblical story is found in Mark 5.)

Surely he took up our infirmities
and carried our sorrows,
yet we considered him stricken by God,
smitten by him and afflicted.
But he was pierced for our transgressions,
He was crushed for our iniquities;
The punishment that brought us peace
Was upon him,
And by his wounds we are healed.
Isaiah 53:4-5

The person diagnosed with terminal cancer, multiple sclerosis, Alzheimer's or some other dreaded affliction lives under a cloud of darkness. As the disease stretches over the body and mind, the cloud grows darker and expands across the horizon of one's life until it covers every moment with its darkness, giving brief and fleeting respite. It is a cloud from which the person cannot escape, except by entering the light. The only light capable of penetrating such darkness comes from the Son. It is a light that at times heals the body and mind but not always. It is a far greater light that allows the person to be free and escape to a land where no such clouds ever appear. Hear his voice and find hope.

Chapter 16

Darkness is no friend to the lonely. Secrecy is just an illusion. When a person is seduced by the siren call of the two joined in whispered chorus there is but one outcome. It would be better to never wake up than to experience the nightmare that comes with dawn's first light. Can anyone count the lonely lives that have been destroyed by the siren call of darkness and secrecy? How many lonely hearts have been seduced by some secret lover to find forbidden, passionate embraces in the night? Lured by the call of temporary passion, many have awakened to the feelings of shame and guilt, never to be the same. Some would say they are the lucky ones since they have escaped their loneliness at least for a short time. Or perhaps they are the tortured ones because they never find freedom from those dark nights of their lives.

How many times had this woman heard the siren call? Why does a woman even listen for it? What emptiness had filled this woman's soul so much that she would be drawn to its call? Perhaps she had heard it many times, whispered in the shadows by many different men. For whatever reason, this woman of secrets found herself with a man on that fateful night. Perhaps she did love him, or perhaps she just wanted to pretend someone loved her. Was this an encounter of the heart with her lover, or was it just another business transaction as she worked the trade of the night? This again is her secret. It is not for us to know.

As the dawn broke and her night came to an end, her secrets were rudely, harshly laid bare. Strange men barged in on her and her lover. How did they know she was there? Did someone betray her? Had someone been spying on her? She shrunk back in terror as the men grabbed for her. Maybe she screamed and fought for her survival, already knowing what fate awaited her. Maybe she buried her face in her hands, filled with shame, not just for being caught, but because she felt the overwhelming guilt of what she had done. Not everyone can understand what this woman of secrets felt that morning because not everyone has had their world come crashing down on them so quickly.

The men drug her outside the room where she and her lover had been. What would happen to her lover? Strangely, they did not grab him, instead they let him go. For some reason they only wanted her. Perhaps he was a friend of one of the men who had intruded into their lives and thus allowed to slink away. Why would he not speak up for her? Why did these men want her? What would happen to her?

The woman of secrets could never have imagined what would soon transpire. While she may have dreaded the fate that judgment would bring her way, she likely would have preferred that to what actually happened. Her guilt and her shame were soon to be paraded before the angry crowds as those indignant men drug her into an open area and threw her down to the ground for all to see.

She could not bear to look up and see the faces of the people staring at her. Most likely she knew some of them. Their eyes surely would not be filled with love or kindness. She could imagine daggers of condemnation and revulsion shooting from their eyes. The woman of secrets did not have to look, she knew her people. If she was going to face her fate, let it come soon, do not drag it out.

As she lay there on the ground, quivering in fear and bemoaning her fate, she heard her accusers.

"We caught this woman in the *act*! We know what the law says we should do, but what do you say we should do?"

Who were they talking to? Who was this that would decide her fate? She could not keep from peeking through the trembling fingers of her hands to see who her judge would be. Nearby stood a man surrounded by a group of other men. She looked to see if she would recognize the man.

You might ask, "Why should she recognize him?"

Some would think a woman of secrets would not be found in the company of such men, men who were respected and who held positions of judging, but such men often know women like her. Many times they are the type of men who use the siren call of darkness and secrecy to lure women into their dark desires. As it turned out, this man who would decide her fate was a stranger to her.

She waited for him to pronounce in righteous indignation, "Stone her! Kill her! Show no mercy!" She knew the men of her community, and they would not tolerate her actions. They would not spare her, and she expected no less from this stranger. She knew the religious leaders of her society had little compassion for the likes of her, because she had heard their sermons many times in her life. If these men put her fate at the feet of this stranger, he must be one of them. Why should she even hope for a different judgment than what would certainly be handed down?

The woman could sense that angry men around her already had chosen their particular weapons of execution. They would stone her on the spot once judgment had been pronounced. What did it feel like to be hit by a rock thrown with the force and the intention to kill? Would it be a sport for those who joined in her execution, with people betting on how many rocks it would take to kill her? Who would draw first blood? Who would strike the lethal blow? How many rocks would have to hit her before she stopped feeling them? Would she be lucky enough to be knocked unconscious by the first blow? She shuddered as she contemplated her impending execution.

The woman of secrets shrank down into the dust and covered her face, fearing the words she would hear next, but there were no words. What was happening? Was he deliberating with his companions about her judgment? What needed to be deliberated? She knew the law. Even she knew there was only one penalty – death by stoning. Perhaps they were just deciding the place and time. That must be it. She peered once more through her fingers to see what was taking place. The man who had become her judge was kneeling near her, drawing something in the dirt with his finger.

People stood there dumbfounded, staring at him. What was he doing? Even the woman of secrets was so shocked that she sat up to watch him. How odd for a judge to act in such a way. Who was this judge that she did not know?

She watched as he slowly stood up to speak. Now would come her judgment. She cowered again. She covered her face and her head with her hands and held her breath, waiting for the first rock to come hurtling in.

"If any of you has never sinned, go ahead and throw the first stone at this woman."

What? Had she heard correctly? She sat up once more and with a befuddled look gazed upon this man who had become her judge. He knelt down again and started writing in the dirt once more with his finger. Her eyes began to widen with astonishment as she began to understand. He was just giving the people time to think about what he said. As his words began to sink in, she noticed a change in the people's faces. They changed from anger and indignation to an uncomfortable guilt as people began to remember what unspeakable things they had done. Then the guilt turned to looks of shame as they thought about what they had almost done. One by one, slowly at first, people began to drop their stones and melt away. It started with the oldest and wisest, but soon enough the angriest ones followed in their tracks as they, too, slinked away in their shame.

Now it was just the woman of secrets, her judge and the companions with him. Who was this man? She watched him rise again and for the first time their eyes met. In his eyes, she saw a look she had never seen before in a man's eyes. They were compassionate; they were tender; they were *pure*. Then she heard her judge speak:

"Where are your accusers, woman? Is there no one here to condemn you for your sin?"

All she could do was whisper with a trembling voice, "No one, sir."

The man reached out for her hand and lifted her up to her feet, and then she heard her kind judge speak again, "Then neither do I condemn you." What judge would say such a thing? How could he be so merciful? She was guilty, and she knew it. There should be some penalty, but he was releasing her, releasing her even from her shame.

"I do not condemn you."

If the judge does not condemn you then who can?

Once more this man spoke to the woman, "Go now and leave your life of sin."

His words were pure. His heart was sincere. His instruction was clear. Whatever had led this woman into a life of secrets would no longer have a hold on her. She was free from her past and free to reclaim a different future. Instead of a judgment of death, this man had given her mercy and a new hope. He saw in her something she had failed to see in herself, and now she must live up to what he saw in her.

Did this woman of secrets realize at that time that the man who spoke for God was the one speaking to her? Perhaps. Sometimes though, people do not realize it has been God's voice they have heard until later. Perhaps this woman of secrets would learn the greatest "secret" – the man who speaks for God also speaks up for people like her.

(This biblical story is found in John 8.)

"What, then, shall we say in response to this? If God is for us, who can be against us? He who did not spare his own Son, but gave him up for us all – how will he not also, along with him, graciously give us all things? Who will bring any charge against those whom God has chosen? It is God who justifies. Who is he that condemns? Christ Jesus, who died – more than that, who was raised to life – is at the right hand of God and is also interceding for us. Who shall separate us from the love of Christ?"
Romans 8:31-35

Whispers and shadows, this is the realm of sin. No one wants to speak of such things. No one wants to admit such things. Those who speak in whispers and seek to live at least partly in the shadows do not want their sins exposed. No matter how hard they try to avoid their fate, they will be exposed. Their exposure will come when it will bring the greatest pain to the most people. No one would ever sin if they ever comprehended the price they would have to pay. Only when the sin has been committed and the price is required do people fully understand. It is at such time that a voice calls out. He still loves. He still forgives. He still offers a new life. Who? It is the voice of the God who continues to speak to us. He speaks to us while we whisper in the shadows. He speaks to us when we have to pay that dreadful price. Those who hear, get another chance. He calls us, hoping we will come. We can come to him as we are, but not to stay as we are. If we will listen, he will help us become more than we have become, more than we ever thought was possible.

Chapter 17

No one really sets out to be brave. It just happens. The brave are people who do what they normally do when the normal gets turned upside down. Bravery comes out when people find themselves at some crisis facing enemies that are greater than them, facing enemies who are seeking to destroy them. At that unexpected moment, the brave are born, not of design but of necessity. They find within their character the ingredients for bravery, and so they become heroes to all who observe.

You may ask, "Who are these brave people, and where do they come from?"

I would answer, "Are they not the same people who live among us that we regard as common? Are they not ordinary people of different ages, genders and races?"

Indeed, it is so. Heroes are not born, they become. Before their acts of bravery, none would have realized they were actually gazing upon heroes. Only afterwards are heroes recognized and sometimes not even then.

There was once a brave young man who lived at a time far removed from us. If you could travel back in time to see this brave young man, you would have missed him. He came from the unlikeliest of places, and he was the unlikeliest of people to become a hero. Yet, his story of bravery has been recorded and passed down through the ages so that we would know about him.

Look back in time, and see a young man sitting near the temple in an ancient city. I suppose he was sitting, for that is often what beggars do when they are looking for help. He was begging because a blind man could do little else to bring in money for his care. I told you that you would not recognize this young man as brave, as a hero.

"What makes a blind beggar so brave?" you may ask.

"Listen to his story and learn."

On that day, this young blind man sat near the temple where people passed by, going back and forth, to and from their way to worship their God. If a beggar wanted to be at a place where help would most likely come, this was the place to sit. People who worship God often show great acts of mercy to those with broken bodies. As he sat there begging from people, unknown to him a particular group of people were walking by and watching him. It was the man who spoke for God and his companions, and as they walked by they were talking about him.

The companions of the man who spoke for God saw the young, blind man begging, and they asked their teacher some very pointed questions, "Why was this man born blind? Was it because he sinned or because his parents sinned?" Such questions are often asked by people with good hearts but limited minds. They need help breaking free of their limits so that they can understand more fully, and so the man who spoke for God taught them.

"This man was born blind for neither reason. In fact, he was born blind for a very special reason. This happened to him so that the work of God could be done in his life."

"What exactly is that work of God?" you may ask.

"That is a good question. Listen to the story and you will learn."

The man who spoke for God went up to the blind man and put some mud on his eyes. He then told the blind man to go to a certain pool and wash away the mud. Then the man who spoke for God moved on while the blind man did as he was told. When the blind man washed the mud from his eyes, a miracle occurred.

"I can see! I can see!"

It was wonderful! This formerly blind man was able to see things he had never before seen in his life. Imagine seeing your first of everything. You see your first colors and you think that green is the most awesome color until you see red, and now red is your favorite until you see royal blue. Who knew there were so many different shades of blue! Imagine seeing what a camel actually looked like! Or imagine seeing the grandeur of the temple for the first time. You sat by it every day for years but had no idea how grand it was. And who knew that there could be so many people and each one look different from the rest. Perhaps your mind would be so overwhelmed from seeing so many new images that you would have to shut your eyes. This surely was the most awesome day of this young man's life.

When this man was able to see, he immediately went home. Imagine the joy in his heart as he *saw* his neighborhood and neighbors for the first time! Who do you think he went home to see? Of course! He went to see his parents, the father and mother who had cared for him all his years. Even after so many centuries have passed, it is not hard to imagine the indescribable happiness that would have filled that family's hearts on that day. Nor is it difficult to see the tears of joy flowing from a mother's eyes or to hear the laughter in a father's heart.

Perhaps the bystanders did not pay much attention at first glance. Perhaps they thought he was just some lunatic who was excited over seeing normal, everyday things. Who gets excited about seeing a cricket? Who screams about seeing a bird in flight?

Who cries over seeing a weed? Even little children don't get excited about such stuff. Only lunatics act like that. Then they started to notice something familiar about this man. Maybe the mother and father were shouting to everyone, "Come see our son! Come see! He sees!" This was no lunatic; this was the blind beggar who sat at the temple. This was the blind boy who had grown up into a blind man in front of their very eyes. They had seen him many times, but how could he see now? What or who had brought about this great miracle?

Soon a crowd of people gathered around this young man who was busy doing nothing more than simply enjoying his first day of seeing. Why were all the people bothering him? They began to argue with each other.

"This is not the blind man."

"Yes, it is the blind man," said some of his neighbors. They surely could not be mistaken because they had seen him daily.

"No, he only looks like him. It is not the same man."

"But I am the blind man. At least I was. Now I am not because I can see."

Well, that was enough for the crowds. They wanted to know how this miracle came about. How does a man born blind now see? This had never happened before.

The young man who had been blind answered them, "The man they call Jesus, the one who claims to speak for God, healed me. He gave me my sight."

Everyone was excited. If the man who spoke for God was here, there might be more miracles. They had missed one, but they would be more alert now. Where is he? No one knew. He had slipped away without notice from anybody.

Had the story ended there, this young man would have gone on with his life, celebrating his miracle. We would say the miracle had happened, and the work of God been done in his life. You would wonder what bravery this young man had shown, because it takes no bravery to be healed.

"Be patient and listen to the rest of the story and you will learn."

The crowds would not leave the young man alone. They took him from his family and his celebration, and they led him to a certain group of people. Those people would weigh in on this miracle and explain how it had come to pass. These people were the religious leaders of their community, and if anyone could explain how a miracle had happened, it would be them. Everyone knew these leaders hated the man who spoke for God and who did these wondrous things among the people. What would they say when they saw this miracle that had been done right under their noses by the very one they hated?

The crowds brought the young man before those enemies of the one who spoke for God. The leaders ordered him to explain what happened so this young man told them his story. These enemies of the one who spoke for God listened and then gruffly said, "This is foolishness. There is no way anyone who claims to speak for God would do this because he did it on the wrong day! He is not from God!"

"The wrong day?" you may ask.

Yes, that was the claim of those who were the enemies of the man who spoke for God because they believed a miracle was work. They also believed that no work should be done on the holy day of each week. The man who claimed to speak for God obviously could not be who he claimed to be if he had done some work on that day.

Some in the crowd did not agree, and they saw an opportunity to further embarrass these enemies of the one who spoke for God.

"How can this man be the evil one you say he is when he gave this blind man his sight? Only God can do such things." This began a great argument between the two sides.

Finally, those enemies of the one who spoke for God told the man who had been born blind to tell them what he thought about the one who had healed him. They would interrogate him to find some weakness in his story, and they would expose him for a fraud. Because they seethed with hatred for the man who spoke with God their thinking had become twisted, and there was no way they would let the story of this miracle stand.

What could this young man say? What did he really know? He was blind when the day started, and now he could see. Why put him on the spot? He did not ask for the miracle and had no part of the dispute between the religious leaders of the community and the man who spoke for God. Whether he liked it or not, though, he had become involved. Now the religious leaders of his community put him on the spot and made him account for the miracle.

The young man looked them in the eye and answered, "I think he must be someone who speaks for God."

"Impossible! We cannot accept that. We need further proof. Besides we do not really know that you were born blind. This whole thing could be a hoax. Send for this young man's parents. Let them verify a miracle has really occurred."

Promptly the young man's parents were summoned.

Every heroic tale has within it the moment when the soon-to-be-hero faces a critical decision and begins to become the hero. When this young man's parents were summoned such a moment occurred for him. This is when you start to see this formerly blind beggar find his bravery, as he becomes the hero of the story. Listen so that you will not miss it.

As you listen, ask yourself, "Who would you expect to stand beside you above all others when no one else will?" Would it not be your parents? Surely your mother will always love you and stand by you? Certainly a father will stand up for his son, unless his son is just a scoundrel. Without a doubt, this young man's parents would not hesitate to stand up for their son.

The young man's parents came when they were summoned. They must have known their son's healing was stirring up excitement and controversy. They knew trouble when they smelled it, and this smelled like trouble. When they were summoned, they came with fear in their hearts. The religious leaders had already decreed that anyone found to be a believer in the man who claimed to speak for God would be an outcast in their community – an outcast, cut off from everyone else, treated like an enemy. Why had they been summoned? They had done nothing wrong. They had not been present when the miracle occurred. They wanted no trouble with anyone. They did not want to be labeled outcasts!

When the parents came to where their son stood among the religious leaders, they hardly had time to notice him. Immediately they were thrown into the middle of the controversy as one of the leaders spoke in a loud, commanding voice that seemed full of self-importance and indignation, "Is this your son? Is it really true that he was born blind? Tell us! And if he was indeed born blind, tell us how it is that he can now see. Answer us!"

As the parents looked at these men who were the enemies of the man who spoke for God, they knew that only one answer would be acceptable to them. Much would be at stake with their answer. Their son looked on and waited for their answer. Up to this point, he had been seemingly unfazed by the controversy that his healing had caused, but now he watched as his parents shuffled their feet and refused to meet his gaze. This was the first day he had ever seen his parents, and now what he saw broke his heart.

"Why are they not happy for me? Why do they have difficulty speaking up for me? I've already answered the questions of these men, why do they hesitate to do the same?"

No son should ever have to see his parents do what his parents did next. His parents, having determined that they did not want to be treated as outcasts even for their own son, composed themselves. They looked away from their son and looked straight at the men who had summoned them.

"He is our son. He was born blind, but how he can see we have no idea. He is old enough to speak for himself. Ask him."

With that they turned their backs on their son and walked off.

Stunned, the young man stood there alone. No longer were his eyes full of joy for all the new things he was seeing. Rather quickly he had learned that sometimes the blind were better off, because they were spared seeing betrayal. Now his gift of sight would always be tainted by the pain of watching his parents abandon him and leave him to stand on his own. Would they ever look him in the eye after that moment?

"They abandoned me! How could they do that to their own son?"

Yet, he did not have much time to ponder his parents' cowardice because soon those enemies were on him again. With newfound fervor and bombast they sought to make the young man cower in fear as they had forced his parents to do. Surely this young man would be easy to break now.

"Alright! Let's get this straight, once and for all. Young man, give glory to God and tell the truth! We know the man you claimed healed you, and we know he is a sinner. Tell us you agree with us."

The young man looked at these intimidating enemies of the man who had given him his sight. He thought of what he had just witnessed in his parents. He knew he stood alone. He knew that he would be even more alone if he did not give the answer these enemies desired. He looked those men in the eyes with his newfound sight and steeled himself with the courage that welled up inside of him. Then he entered the fray with full force.

"A sinner? Well, isn't that something. I cannot answer that, but I can tell you this – I was blind, but now I see."

"Tell us what this man did to you. How did he give you sight? Answer us!"

"I already told you once. Why do you want me to tell you again? Do you want to become his disciples, too?"

You could see the defiance in his eyes when he asked this last question. It was his way of saying to these enemies that he would not cower. He was indeed his own man. He would stand up to them and give an answer. He felt no fear of them.

"Enough! We have had enough from your smart mouth. You are an ignorant fool!"

History does not record for us the actual words these enemies said to this brave young man, but it was likely something of the sort that you do not repeat so you and I are spared their vulgar anger.

The brave young man was not finished though, in fact he was just getting started.

"Well, isn't this a sight to behold! Everybody knows that God does not listen to sinners. You yourselves claim that, but here I am standing before you – proof that God has listened to this man who speaks for him. What happened to me is unheard of and you know it! This man could never have done this if he did not truly speak for God!"

With that response, the brave young man had given his final answer, and he knew what his public defiance would cost him.

"That is it! We will hear no more. You yourself are a sinner. That is all you have ever been. You are now an outcast. Throw him out!"

Such treatment might have caused a lesser man to walk away dejected, filled with self-pity and despair, but it does not affect the brave in that way. This young man had shown himself to be full of bravery. He had stood alone, but he had stood up to the attack. Now as he walked away, this brave man was still standing.

It was after he walked away that he again encountered the man who had healed him. The one who spoke for God had heard that his enemies had thrown the young man out. He deliberately sought after the young man until he found him. Why had the one who spoke for God walked away in the first place? Why did he not hang around and answer his enemies' questions for himself? Was the one who spoke for God afraid of his enemies? Why did he want the young man to stand alone in that ordeal? Why was he coming back to the young man? Was there something still to be done?

"There must be more to the story," you may say, and you are right.

"Listen and you will learn."

What was the greatest miracle that occurred on that day? It may surprise you that it was not about a blind man getting his sight. It was something far greater and far more precious. When the one who spoke for God found the young man, he asked him, "Do you believe in the one who claims to come from God?"

The brave young man answered, "If you tell me who he is, I will believe in him."

"It is me."

When the brave young man heard this, he fell down and worshipped the one who came to him from God and said, "I believe in you, Lord."

Now the work of God was done. It had only started when the one who spoke for God had given the blind man his sight. It continued when the young man found the courage in himself to stand up for the truth even when he stood alone. It was finished when the young man believed in the one who had healed him and called him Lord.

(This biblical story is found in John 9.)

"Then they asked him, 'What must we do
to do the works God requires?'"
"Jesus answered, 'The work of God is this:
to believe in the one he has sent.'"
John 6:28-29

"Ah! Now I see!" you say, and so you may, but some people are still blind even today. Some people see with their eyes, but they do not have the faith to see this one who spoke for God. He is still working today, speaking to people so that all the blind may see and believe.

Chapter 18

The man who spoke for God encountered many people from all walks of life. As he traveled to the various towns, people sought him out. Some sought him because they needed his help. They knew someone who was sick and perhaps the man who spoke for God would perform a miracle of healing. Some sought him out because they loved to hear the things he would say about God. He gave them hope and a sense of peace. Such words were good news to people who had long been oppressed. Others who sought the man who spoke for God did so for less noble reasons. Then there were others who were drawn to him for more personal and private reasons.

There was a preacher who lived in a certain town who had heard about the man who spoke for God. The preacher thought it would be good to have the man who spoke for God as a guest in his home since he was held in high honor by the people. Surely that honor would rub off on the one with whom he chose to eat a meal. When the opportunity arrived, the preacher extended an invitation to the man who spoke for God, and to his great delight, his invitation was accepted.

Oh, this would be a grand occasion! The preacher invited many guests so that the people could see him and the man who spoke for God conversing about weighty matters. He would surely be seen as important by all the people. If the people listened to the man who spoke for God, surely they would listen to the preacher after all this took place. He had hosted many important people in his home before, but none like the man who spoke for God, so the preacher busied himself with his preparations and had his servants prepare the meal and the table.

Soon enough his very special guest arrived along with his disciples and with the other guests. The preacher was filled with excitement as surely were the other people. Perhaps there would be some miracle that would transpire. What a sermon illustration that would be! Perhaps the preacher envisioned how he might use such a story in one of his upcoming sermons:

"I am reminded of the time when the man who speaks for God came to *my* house. As we sat side by side discussing the deep things of God, we were approached by a man in great need…"

Yes, what a powerful sermon that would be! People would hang on his every word.

Still, there might not be a miracle. No matter, because the man who spoke for God would surely have something insightful to say. Maybe the preacher would agree with him and be seen as a friend of the man who spoke for God. Or maybe he would not agree, and then the preacher would have his opportunity to challenge him. If so, the preacher could gain great honor for himself as the one who bested the man who *claimed* to speak for God. Yes, this was a marvelous opportunity for the preacher.

When Jesus arrived, the preacher seated everyone around the table for the meal. It would be a great event as everyone reclined around the table to eat and discuss. In those days people reclined at the table when they ate a meal. They leaned on pillows or cushions towards the table as their feet extended outwards from the table.

The preacher gladly welcomed his guests, but he was not really concerned about any of them. He did not even offer his guests the most basic courtesy of his home. In those days, people traveled by foot on dirt roads. Since they wore sandals, their feet would get dusty from their travels. Whenever guests entered someone's home, the host would at least provide a bowl of water and a towel for them to wash and dry their feet. The preacher did not offer such hospitality to the man who spoke for God or to any of his other guests. After all, this meal wasn't really about them. Far weightier matters consumed the preacher's thinking, and he did not have time to be concerned about other people's feet.

Once everyone had been seated, the meal progressed just as the preacher expected. Perhaps the preacher reveled in his self-importance as the man who spoke for God engaged him in conversation. Perhaps, as the preacher talked with his guest, his eyes darted around to see if others noticed. Maybe he did not even really listen to the words the man who spoke for God said. Maybe he was more concerned with how he would respond so that he would impress those who would hear. Perhaps he would even impress the man who claimed to speak for God.

It was at this time that the preacher's efforts were completely undone by the most unlikely person. A woman, of all people, who lived in that town, had heard that the man who spoke for God would be at the preacher's house for a meal that day. This woman had a dark past. There were things about her that everybody knew. People looked down on her and scorned her. The woman really did not mind what people thought of her because she was consumed with her own feelings of guilt and shame. She knew she was a horrible person who deserved everyone's scorn. The woman also knew that she was not invited to the preacher's house and would not be welcomed if she went. Going would invite more scorn and rejection upon her, perhaps even by the preacher.

Still, this woman felt compelled to be with the man who spoke for God. She had heard of him and perhaps had even heard him speak of the things of God. She knew he was a man who spoke for God and that she was a woman whom God would surely despise. None of that mattered because she had to go to him. She could not stay away, and so she went to the preacher's house, too.

The preacher did not see her until it was too late; after all, he was too busy posturing and looking important to notice someone like this woman. By the time the preacher saw the woman, he could not stop the events that unfolded. The woman had worked her way gingerly through the crowd and entered into the preacher's home. Then she worked her way around to the man who spoke for God. There she stood behind him. She had a reason, her reason, for being there. She wanted to show her love by anointing him with some very expensive perfume, but now that she was there, she was overwhelmed. She was overwhelmed with her own dark past.

As she stood behind the man who spoke for God, she started to weep. At first the tears came slowly, but soon she wept uncontrollably. She could not stop weeping. As she stood behind the man who spoke for God, her streams of tears began to fall on his feet. The man who spoke for God turned to gaze upon this woman. At that point she fell at his feet.

Her reason for being there was to honor him. This woman who had a dark past that everyone knew had come to anoint the man who spoke for God with some perfume. She knew her dark past, and she knew she was not worthy to touch someone like the man who spoke for God, but she could not hold herself back. She fell at his feet, and as she poured perfume on him, her tears continued to fall on his feet. His feet were soaked now, so she took her hair and let it hang free. She then used her own hair as a towel to dry his feet. Not only did she do this, she also kissed the feet of the man who spoke for God over and over again. She could say no words to explain her actions. What she felt in her heart could not be explained by words. No one there could recall ever seeing such a thing before.

The man who spoke for God did not say a word either. He simply allowed the woman to wash his feet with her tears and dry them with her hair. He watched her pour the perfume on his feet, and he watched her kiss his feet repeatedly with her lips. No one had ever treated him with such love, love that came from deep brokenness and humility of spirit.

However, not everyone was touched by the woman's display of humility and love. The preacher had noticed, and he had a different opinion. He thought to himself:

"This man cannot be someone who speaks for God. If he was such a man, he would know this woman's dark past, and he would not even let this woman touch him."

Perhaps the preacher thought of what he would say to such a woman if he were ever approached by her. Maybe he recalled a time when he had stood proudly and, proclaiming to speak for God himself, had cast this woman out of his church because of her shameful and dark past. Such women did not belong in a house of God. Whatever he was thinking, the preacher now looked in disdain on this woman and also on the man who claimed to speak for God. He had already judged them both in his mind.

Then the man who spoke for God turned to the preacher and spoke to *him*. He told the preacher a very simple story of forgiveness. It was the story of two men, one who owed a great debt and one who owed a small debt. These debts were owed to the same man and both debts were forgiven.

The man who spoke for God asked the preacher, "Who will love the man who forgave their debts more?"

The preacher knew the answer as did all his guests. Lest he be seen as a fool and lose all credibility, he was compelled to answer.

"The one who had been forgiven the most."

Even as he answered the man who spoke for God, the preacher knew that the story would not turn out well for him, and indeed it did not.

The man who spoke for God replied to the preacher, "When I came into your home you did not offer me even the smallest courtesy of providing a bowl of water and a towel so that I could wash my feet. But this woman with the dark past that you look down on has done much more. With her own tears and hair she has washed my feet. She has poured perfume on my feet and continues to kiss them with her lips. She has shown me love, you have not. Therefore, all the sins of her past that she has carried the shame and guilt of have been forgiven her." Then instead of treating this woman with scorn, the man who spoke for God offered her love. He sent her away with peace and hope.

The woman with the dark past knew this was something far more than she deserved. However, this was her good news. She had learned that God loved people like her, even though she was unworthy. She had learned that God wanted her and loved her, because the man who spoke for God had forgiven her. Surely she wept tears of joy as she left the preacher's house.

What became of the preacher? No one knows any more. Perhaps he saw how he was wrong, and perhaps he changed. Maybe he began to love others in his community who had their own dark pasts. It could be that he even recognized that he had his own dark past and that he, too, needed forgiveness from God. Perhaps on that day his tears flowed as well. Maybe on that day he began to really be a good preacher and speak more accurately for the God for whom he claimed to speak.

We can only hope.

(This biblical story is found in Luke 7.)

Create in me a pure heart, O God,
and renew a steadfast spirit within me.
Do not cast me from your presence
or take your Holy Spirit from me.
Restore to me the joy of your salvation
and grant me a willing spirit, to sustain me.

Then I will teach transgressors your ways,
and sinners will turn back to you.
Save me from bloodguilt, O God,
the God who saves me,
and my tongue will sing of your righteousness.
O Lord, open my lips,
and my mouth will declare your praise.
You do not delight in sacrifice, or I would bring it;
you do not take pleasure in burnt offerings.
The sacrifices of God are a broken spirit;
a broken and contrite heart,
O God, you will not despise.
Psalm 51:10-17

Murderers. Domestic Abusers. Terrorists. Idolaters. Adulterers. Homosexuals. Rapists. Molesters. People addicted to pornography. Prostitutes. Strippers. Pimps. Abortionists. Those who have had abortions. Liars. Racists. Reverse Racists. Gamblers. Greedy. Alcoholics. Drunks. Shoplifters. Thieves. Embezzlers. Drug addicts. Gang members. Criminals of the worst sort. Heartless. Cruel. Selfish. Inventors of evil. Sinners of all sorts. No one has to tell us these are wrong. We already know. Maybe tears are streaming down our cheeks as we see ourselves in this sinful woman. When does our dark side make us unlovable to God? Never. God calls all people to turn from the darkness and turn towards him so that he can love them all.

Chapter 19

Many a night the man who spoke for God had laid his head down on a strange bed. He was a traveler. He loved seeing the different places, but mostly, he loved meeting new people and spending time with them. He was definitely a people person, in an odd sort of way. He loved people, but they did not always like him in return. Some of them thought him a little strange. His own family, whom he loved, even thought he was crazy. Few people really understood him. Even some of his closest friends thought him to be a bit odd. When you are a people person, it can be hard on you to be misunderstood so often.

His life was not easy. He often rose earlier than his companions and often stayed up later, long past the hour everyone else had fallen asleep. While others could go home to family, he did not. He had long since left home. Now he was a traveler, always going from one place to the next, because he knew he had to keep busy. Too many people depended upon him, and his time was short. There was no time to slow down.

This traveler stayed on the road, going from one town to the next. Sometimes people were kind to him and welcomed him into their homes for the night, but he would get up early to carry on with his work the next day. He had come to accept his life. It could be harsh and wearisome at times, actually much of the time, but it was the life he chose. Though hard, his life was filled with purpose; he was happy with his life.

Along the way, this man who spoke for God made some special friends – a family in a small town tucked in the mountains. Ah! It was a beautiful place to be sure, but the scenery did not draw him there. Something special about the family attracted him. They were so dear to him, even though he had not known them long. Sometimes one is fortunate and finds such friends. You meet them once, and you know they will be true friends for life. This family, a brother and his two sisters, had become such for him.

He liked stopping in their home on every opportunity that he could, but his work did not allow that much time to visit them. When he was in the area, he loved to stay in their home. In some ways, staying at their house was better than having his own home. He found laughter, joy and companionship there. He could talk with them about matters on his heart, and they were willing to listen. They seemed to understand him. Perhaps that was what drew this constant traveler so tightly to this family.

It came about that during his travels word was sent to him that his dear friend, the brother had fallen sick. The traveler's friends immediately began to gather their things so that they would be ready for a quick trip to that home tucked away in the mountains. They waited on the traveler with growing impatience.

"Hurry, we must leave now."

The saddened traveler did not get up to go, however. He just sat still and remained calm.

Perhaps he was praying for his friend, or maybe he was considering whether he should go or not. It was no secret that, in his work, he had made many enemies as he traveled around the country. Perhaps he should not make this journey because it may not be safe.

What did they do? They sat. They sat for two days, doing nothing.

The companions of the man who spoke for God finally decided they would not be going to see his friend. Then on that second day, the man who spoke for God got up in the morning and told everybody to get ready to travel again. They were going.

"Why now? Perhaps we should lay low a little longer. Today is not a good day to die," his companions said.

However, he insisted they take this journey; they must go and go now.

"Very well. Perhaps today is a good day to die after all."

This journey was different than others. The traveler's companions were sad and afraid. As they journeyed, the man who spoke for God told them something strange. He knew that his friend had already died. Then why were they going? Would they not put themselves in danger and die alongside their friend by continuing on their journey to the small town tucked away in the mountains? It did not make sense.

As they came close to the town, people ran to tell the sisters that the man who spoke for God had come. Immediately, the older sister ran to meet him. She fell at his feet weeping when she came to her friend. Her heart was overwhelmed by the death of the brother she deeply loved. The man who spoke for God tried to offer her words of comfort and encouragement. He tried to give her hope. He came to help, but in her grieving this sister did not understand, she only knew that she missed her brother. They had always been close. Her brother had taken her in and cared for her. His home had been her home, but now he was no more.

"Why didn't you come when we sent for you? You have healed others. You could have saved him."

The older sister did not intend to burden or accuse the traveler, but her grieving heart compelled her to pour out her anguish to this man who had become such a dear friend. Her great pain cried out for release. She struggled to understand how her brother's death had come to be. Her brother and the man who spoke for God were good friends. He could have healed her brother with just a word. He had done as much for strangers. Why had he ignored their cry for help?

"Don't worry," her friend said to her. "Your brother will be fine. He will live again."

In her tears and anguish, the older sister did not understand what her friend meant. Her brother was dead! She had expected more than some religious rhetoric. She had expected the man who spoke for God to come and heal her brother before it was too late. Now it was too late. Her brother was dead, and it did not have to be since the one who spoke for God could have traveled to their home and healed him.

"He's dead!" her spirit wanted to scream out.

In her grief and agony, the older sister felt something happen inside her though. She began to be calm as her friend touched her and walked with her. She began to listen to his words and recalled the many times she had heard him speak for God. She had believed in him then, and even though she did not understand, she would believe in him now. That was one reason why the man who spoke for God loved this family so much. They trusted him.

The older sister went home to tell her younger sister about the arrival of their friend. The younger sister, upon hearing about their friend's arrival, also ran out to meet him. She went to him, fell at his feet and spoke the only words her broken spirit could utter:

"Lord, if you have been here, my brother would not have died."

The traveler's heart wrenched in agony for his friends. The deepest part of his being ached for them. Yet, the man who spoke for God had come at this time for a reason. He had come to show his dearest friends, and all who watched, something special. They would witness something they had never seen before.

He asked them, "Where is my friend?"

As they took him to see his friend, his heart felt overwhelmed, and he wept. What would make the one who speaks for God cry? What would make the one who knew everything weep? Tears of love, for as he saw his friends' tears flow, his began to flow with them. They hurt, so he hurt. When his travels had brought him from the far reaches of his Father's home, had he known then that he would hurt so much for one family? Did he know his heart would break because of their sorrow? As they wept, the man who spoke for God also wept. Oh, how he wept!

What was he going to do? When they got to the burial site, he told them to open the tomb, "Move the stone from the entrance."

"But he has been dead for *four days!*"

The man who spoke for God did not heed their objection; he would not be put off from his mission. Yes, he could have come earlier and saved his friend when he was only sick, but he would now do something far greater. Through him, people would see the glory of the God who loves all people. The man who spoke for God began to speak to him now in prayer. Then he called out to the dead man in the grave!

"Come out! Wake up, friend!"

Every eye watched the entrance of the grave. What would happen? Had they heard what they thought they had heard? Was the man who spoke for God serious? Could he bring the dead back to life?

Yes! There he was. The dead man lived! He was all bundled up as he walked out of the tomb, but he was alive!

"He's alive!"

The tears suddenly stopped as people were in shock and in awe. How great was God to do something like this! People shouted and celebrated. The sisters rushed up and hugged their brother. Then the tears started to flow again, tears of sheer ecstasy.

Perhaps the man who spoke for God shed a few more tears himself for the people he loved, and he dearly loved these friends. Perhaps now he could go home with them and enjoy their company once more.

As you ponder this story, remember that one day it will be your body that lies in a grave. One day your body will sleep as it waits for the one who will call all people. On that day, the man who speaks for God will call your name, and you will rise from the grave. On that day, if you have listened to his voice, you too will be given a new life.

(This biblical story is found in John 11.)

"Since the children have flesh and blood, he too
shared in their humanity so that by his death he
might destroy him who holds the power of death –
that is the devil – and free those who all their lives
were held in slavery by their fear of death.
For surely it is not angels he helps but
Abraham's descendants."
Hebrews 2:14-16

Why do people fear death? It is a destiny we all have in common. No one can avoid it, but we hang on tenaciously to life, no matter what it looks like, no matter how difficult it may be. We have made strong attachments to people. There are things we want to do, places we want to go and experiences we want to go through. However, at some point it all has to end. It cannot last. Our bodies are proof that we cannot go on. As we age, our bodies inevitably move towards the day of our death. Our only hope is to look beyond that day to the resurrection and to the Lord of the resurrection. Hear his voice and know there is a greater life. The friend of the man who spoke for God ultimately had to die again, but his next resurrection will be one that will take him into life everlasting. This is the life that God calls all people to. When we hear and answer him, we have no more reason to fear death.

Chapter 20

Who cares about the wealthy? Oh, many people do when they want their money. "Friends" are plentiful for the wealthy, but who really cares for them? When churches reach out to the communities surrounding them, they are often drawn to ministering to the poor and the wretched. Perhaps they take too much for granted when considering the rich. Perhaps they do not understand the brokenness of the rich. Who speaks to the rich the words of God that will meet them in their brokenness and bring healing to their souls? Who indeed? Perhaps we all need to hear this particular story again.

"What story?" you may ask.

"It is a story that has been told for many centuries now, the story of one particular rich man whose life was not as it seemed. Listen to his story now and understand the brokenness of the rich."

The story begins with a dream, maybe a simple hope. Two parents had a boy, a boy in whom they placed great expectations. They gave him a name which had a special meaning. His name meant "innocent, pure, righteous." Perhaps it was just a family name; regardless, it was a powerful name for this boy to live up to. This boy came from a great line of people with a heritage rooted in people who walked with God. His ancestors included the likes of Abraham, Isaac and Jacob, as well as Moses, Joshua and King David. He belonged to a people chosen by God himself. This young boy had been born into a nation with a strong heritage that clearly set his identity. Indeed he had much to live up to if he were to live up to his name.

Unfortunately, we do not know much of his early story other than that. It is not until he was in the middle of his own story that we hear of him. He had grown into a man of short stature but had accumulated great wealth, probably having more money than he could spend in a lifetime. With that wealth would have come a nice house and servants to take care of him and any need he had. It would seem that this man lived a wonderful life; however, it may surprise you to find out that his life was anything but wonderful. Wealth had exacted a terrible price from him.

"Why do I say this, and how do I know it?"

In his story we are told how he achieved his great wealth. We are not told when he chose his career path or what prompted his particular choice. We are simply told that he was a tax collector. To be more exact, he was a chief tax collector. In such an office, he had to collect taxes from his own people to support the cruel, foreign government that now ruled over his people. Collecting taxes for the far away king was really a rather simple business. Promise the king more money than someone else promised. Once he gave you the position, hire some thugs (that is, some associates) to collect those taxes for you. In fact, they could collect more than promised to the king. The king did not care as long as he received what had been promised to him. This "extra" tax was the chief tax collector's pay, and he made sure he was paid very well. He became wealthy on the pain and suffering of his own people.

For his people this was nothing less than betrayal. Instead of living up to his name, this man had chosen to become rich at the cost of giving up his identity. He turned his back on his own people and joined the ranks of an oppressive regime. This man was anything but pure and righteous. He was no child of Abraham.

We can imagine how his parents must have felt, if they were still living, as they heard about their son's business dealings:

"Let me tell you what your son did to my family today!"

"What did you teach your son when he was growing up? How could you have raised such a horrible son?"

"Your son took our last bit of money today. My children are starving, and he sent his thugs to take everything. What will my children eat now?"

"May God bring on you the misery your son has brought on us! You deserve whatever punishment God brings upon your head!"

As terrible as the life of the parents must have been, even more so was it with the son himself. He had wealth but no friends, no real friends anyway. His relationship with his parents and his extended family was broken. He had broken trust with them and with his community. He was an enemy among his own people. In reality, he had no people. He was a wealthy loner. That was his identity now. He had turned his back on all that had identified him. He no longer thought of himself as a child of Abraham. He had long ago given up any thought of being innocent and pure. His bank account was full, but his heart and his spirit were bankrupt. Riches could not fill the emptiness in his soul.

"Why do I have to feel so empty inside? Why can I not be happy in my wealth?"

There were no answers to these questions that plagued him. Whenever such thoughts came upon him, he had learned to bury them and go about his business. Whenever he overheard someone's insults, he ignored them. He told himself that he did not care, but his unhappiness was boiling up underneath the façade and the lies he told himself. Unless something changed he would implode, and his life would crumble underneath him.

Then one day, a strange man began to dominate the news. People began to talk about a man just to the north who lived out in the wilderness. He was a preacher. This man talked tirelessly about the coming of the kingdom of God. The preacher talked of one greater than himself who would come after him, a man who would speak for God. Many people in this short, rich man's country went out to hear this preacher. Many realized the wickedness of their choices and how it would cause them to miss out on the kingdom that was coming. Even a great number of fellow tax collectors went to hear the preacher. It seems this chief tax collector was not the only one with a guilty conscience, but at this time, he was not interested in hearing some hairy, wild-eyed preacher.

However, a couple of years later, opportunity knocked once more. While going about his business, this short tax collector noticed an unusual excitement among the people of his city. He could not recall seeing the people so stirred up before. He knew of no celebration on the city docket. Such news would always be relayed to him, and he had heard nothing about any such activities in the city. What had stirred up the crowds so?

He started to inquire of the people, hoping for an answer. Normally, he hated the idea of asking people for information. It would give them an opportunity to say something cruel, and even worse, it made him feel inferior. However, he found himself increasingly eager to discover the root of the people's excitement and joy. Electricity filled the air as people anticipated something great, and he must not miss out on whatever would happen.

As he asked around, someone mentioned that the man who speaks for God was nearby, and everyone was going to see him.

"The man who speaks for God? Is he really nearby?" The short, little man had heard the stories of the one who spoke for God. "What brings him here?"

As this short, little man recalled the stories, his curiosity began to rise. He had heard that the one who spoke for God did things nobody had ever seen before. He had performed many miracles of healing, doing things that doctors could not do. There were rumors that he had even raised people from the dead. He knew those had to be exaggerations, but what if he did some miracle here in his city? That would be surely worth some entertainment for the day. Perhaps, just maybe, some deeper desire stirred within the heart of this short, little man. Maybe a troubled heart looked for peace. Whatever the reason was that motivated him, he followed the crowd to this man of God to see what he could see.

Following hurriedly along, he soon came to the place where the man who spoke for God was surrounded by a large crowd of people.

"The crowd is too large, the people too many, and I am too short to see over them!"

He could not see the man. He cursed being so short. Now the man who speaks for God was on the move, but not very far down the road was a tree that he could climb.

"If I run fast enough, perhaps nobody would notice me climbing up the tree."

The crowds seemed more interested in the man who spoke for God anyway. Surely no one would see him climbing into the tree.

The short, little man ran down the road and proceeded to climb. He did not know what he expected to see or hear. It was said that this man who speaks for God said marvelous things that stirred people's hearts and calmed their spirits. It was said that he spoke not just to the minds of the people but also to their souls. If he did not see a miracle, perhaps he might catch some interesting teaching or a bit of conversation that the man of God might have with the other people. His curiosity drew him to the man of God and drove him up that tree.

He could see the man who spoke for God coming closer. He tried to hide behind the leaves and sit as still as he could, hoping no one would notice him. He certainly did not want to draw attention to himself. He would be the laughingstock of the city if people saw him up in the tree.

The man who spoke for God drew closer. He was almost to the tree. Thoughts raced through the short little man's mind with each step taken by this man.

"Be still and don't move. What is he saying? Oh, no! Why is he stopping? He's looking up. No! Don't look up! Why did I climb up into this tree? Please, don't see me!"

The man who spoke for God did see. Not only did he see, but he stopped to speak to the short, little man in the tree.

"Come down. I want to go to your house."

The short, little tax collector couldn't believe what he had just heard. At first he was embarrassed when people saw him up in the tree, but now he did not care. The man who spoke for God was speaking to him and wanted to go home with him.

"Why?"

"Who cares!" and to his home they went – a short, little man that nobody in the city liked and the man who spoke for God.

Of course, this short, little man invited others to come along. The man who spoke for God came with his companions. The short, little tax collector nobody liked threw a great feast, and that day truly turned into a day of celebration. Those who were there had a wonderful time, as did he. He and his special guest talked. He could not get enough of his words; he wanted more. For the first time in his life, his heart was full. The feelings of emptiness that had plagued him for so long had vanished. He began to see himself differently. He was no longer a lost man deserving of people's hate and disgust. He was better than that. He was better than anyone thought, even better than he himself thought.

He also began to see the people around him differently as he listened to the words spoken by this messenger of God. These people were not his enemies. They were his friends. He had treated them as nothing more than a source of income and wealth, but they were his neighbors. His heart began to open up to them, and as he saw them anew, he saw himself anew. He looked at himself and the people of the city through the eyes of the man who spoke for God and became a different man. He now understood what he had done to the people, how he had hurt and oppressed many of them.

"How can I undo all the wrong that I have done to so many?"

He did not know if he could even recount all the wrong he had done and everyone whom he had wronged. Was it even possible to undo all the wrong and soothe the pain he had caused?

"It does not matter! Something has to be done!"

Right then and there, in the presence of the man who spoke for God and all in his house, the short, little man made a pledge.

"I will give half of my wealth to the poor. Half of it all! On top of that, I will pay back anybody that I have wronged. In fact, I will pay them back more than what I have taken from them, four times as much! Yes, that is what I will do!"

All of the people were astounded. They had not liked this man for so long that they could not believe what their ears had just heard. They had never believed it was possible for him to change. At first no one knew what to say. Such dramatic change taking place so quickly was like a miracle had happened.

Then the man who spoke for God said the most incredible thing to the short, little man that nobody had liked.

"Today salvation has come into this home for this man is a child of Abraham! He was lost, and I came to save him!"

At that moment, with those words, this man regained his heritage. At that moment he became the pure, innocent and righteous man his parents had envisioned.

What a story!

(This biblical story is found in Luke 19.)

Jesus said to him, "Today salvation has come into this house, because this man, too, is a son of Abraham. For the Son of Man came to seek and save what was lost."
Luke 19:8-10

If we knew on the day we were born what would be written on the pages of our lives, would we not start our lives with regret? If we could look at those pages and see the bad decisions and choices we would make, we would surely try to rip those pages out. If we could foresee how our lives would be littered with failures that we brought upon ourselves, we might try to climb back into our mothers' wombs. It is a good thing we cannot read the pages before they are written, but written they will be. After they are written, we will then be able to read about our bad decisions and failures, and we will re-live the pain. We will not want to do so, but each written page carries memories that cannot be easily erased. It is for that reason many people turn to the one who speaks for God. He does not wipe away the memories, but he helps people overcome them. He offers them the direction and the opportunities to change the direction of their life stories. He gives them hope for better futures that will far outshine their pasts.

Chapter 21

Why do many men think following the one who spoke for God is just a women's religion? Do they not realize that from the very beginning great men have followed the one who came from God? While women are definitely precious and important people in the kingdom, there is a valued place for men as well. Many men have followed the one who came from God and have shown great valor and courage in doing so. In fact, they have shown more valor and courage than many other men who have lived and died for lesser causes. Keep this in mind as you hear the story of a man called Rock.

Some men seem to be born leaders. They exude confidence and self-assurance. They look rugged, and they do the kind of work that rugged men do. When some crisis arises, people automatically look to such men for guidance. These men can rally people to what seems like a lost cause and stir them up to do great things. They never lack for something to say when something needs to be said, and they back their words up with action. Rock was just such a man.

Even though Rock was a leader of men, he traveled a road more unusual than even he expected. The journey down this challenging road shaped him into an even greater leader, the type of leader he never thought or dreamed of becoming. To become such a leader he first had to travel the road of a follower. He followed the man who claimed to speak for God. He followed him for three years to make sure he knew for certain this man really did speak for God. Many men had died when they made such a commitment to the wrong leader. However, Rock was not afraid to die and would gladly do so, if he knew this man was indeed from God.

This future leader of men listened and watched the one who claimed to speak for God for those three years. He saw the miracles. He even became part of one miracle, once walking on water with the man who spoke for God. He listened to his teachings, and slowly, he came to believe in him. He did not understand him fully. In truth no one seemed to, not even those who were among his closest companions.

One day, this man from God asked them, "Who does everybody say that I am? Tell me, what do you hear?"

They answered, "Everybody thinks you are one of the prophets who has come back, but they are not sure which one."

Then he asked them, "Well, who do you think I am?"

To no one's surprise, Rock had an immediate answer.

"You are the one who has been sent from God."

Oh, how great that made the man from God feel! He had worked long and hard for these men to understand. And they did understand – until the one sent from God spoke again.

"I must tell you now that we are going to the Great City. When we get there, I am going to be handed over, and I will be killed."

"No way! Absolutely not! You cannot die just when we started to believe in you. This is not the way this is supposed to work!"

These words came from Rock as he shouted at the one he had come to believe in. He was stunned by the remarks of the one he now knew had been sent from God. He would have said more, but the one who spoke for God rebuked him in a way that cut to his heart and silenced him.

"Get behind me, Satan! You do not have in mind the things of God. I will not let you cause me to fail."

This rebuke hit him like a blow from a hammer, and immediately silenced Rock. He did not know what to say; he was confused. Only later would he understand how much the one sent from God did not want to die. If he had only understood, he never would have put such a tempting thought before the one he followed.

The days to come were busy with activity, excitement and anxiety. The anxiety grew as they drew closer to the Great City. They could see it in the face of the one they had come to believe in and now followed. It was in each one of the companions as well. They watched as the crowds cheered the one sent from God and called him king. How strange it felt to watch this celebration and watch the one they followed weep at the same time. As they went up the mountain into the Great City, they sensed conflict was unavoidable and imminent.

Soon they ate one last special meal together. It was a holy meal whose significance increased as the meal progressed, and as the one they believed in talked to them. At one point the one who came from God spoke to the man called Rock.

"I have been praying for you. Satan wants you. This very night you will deny me – not once, not twice but three times."

"Me? Deny you? Never! I will die for you. In fact, I have a sword. Indeed we have two swords!"

These words stunned Rock as much as the rebuke he had received a few days earlier. No one had ever questioned his loyalty. Surely the one he now followed knew his commitment was genuine. The one who spoke for God seemed to know everything. It was he who saw his strength and gave Rock his name. Now that he believed, there was no power that could shake him and cause him to deny his leader. Rock meant every word he said; he would die before he would deny. He would he live up to his name and stand firm and true.

Thinking such things and speaking bold words in an upper room is one thing, but living up to them is quite another. He bore the qualities of a leader, but tonight he would discover if he would follow. What kind of follower would Rock really turn out to be? Would he live up to the name given him by the one who spoke for God? Would he become the leader he believed he could be? The dark events that would soon unfold would reveal the answers to those questions.

That evening they went off to a garden. The one who spoke for God requested that three disciples follow him further into the garden to pray with Him. He did not want to be alone at this time. Again to no one's surprise, Rock was one of those chosen to go. He went along, and he tried to pray, but he kept falling asleep. No matter how hard he tried, he kept falling asleep. His spirit wanted to answer the call of his master, but he was just so tired. The events of the week and the late hour had caught up with him. Even when the one who spoke for God pleaded with them to stay awake and pray for him, he could not prevent the inevitable – he succumbed to his weariness and slept once more.

He was at last awakened by a commotion. A mob of angry men approached. They came to seize the one he followed.

"Where is that sword?"

Rock reached for it and struck out at one of the mob. They would not seize the one he had come to believe in without a fight. He slashed off one man's ear. As he drew back to strike again, the one who spoke for God stopped him and rebuked him one more time.

"What? Will he not let me fight for him even now?"

He did not know what to do. He stood ready to fight, and he would place himself between the mob and the one he followed. He would give his life for the one who spoke for God, but he had just been forbidden from striking again. For a moment he stood there dazed and confused as the one who spoke for God restored the ear of the man that Rock had just struck. Then the one called Rock ran away, and all the others followed suit. They left the one for whom they had pledged to die to meet his fate alone.

No one knows where they all went that night with each fleeing to his own particular place of safety, but the man called Rock could not stay away. He gathered himself and reigned in his fears and followed his leader who was now at the mercy of the arresting mob. He kept his distance to avoid being seen. The one who spoke for God was taken before the leading council and the temple leaders. Rock stood in a courtyard nearby, warming himself near a fire alongside some others.

Suddenly a woman asked him, "You are one of his followers, aren't you? You followed the man who is standing on trial right over there, didn't you?"

"No! You are mistaken. I did not follow him," the man called Rock said.

A little bit later, a girl noticed him and blurted out to those standing nearby, "I saw this man with the one that claims to be from God. He is one of his followers."

"No! I swear to you I am not one of his followers!" Rock protested as he became increasingly agitated.

However, those standing by him would not let the accusation rest.

"You surely are one of his followers. Even your accent gives you away."

At that point, the man called Rock could take no more and, cursing himself, yelled, "I tell you I never knew that man who claims to be from God!"

Then Rock heard it. Perhaps most people did not notice it that night, but he did. It happened just as the man from God said it would. A rooster crowed! He had denied his Lord – not once, not twice but three times. It had happened just as the one he believed in had said. Even now, Rock could see the man who spoke for God standing not too far away. When he heard the rooster crow, the disciple called Rock looked at the one he had denied. He was horrified at what he had just done, and then the one who spoke for God turned his head and looked him in the eye. Rock was so ashamed as his eyes met the eyes of the one whom he had just denied.

The man called Rock fled. He felt as if a giant hammer had just pounded him into sand. He was no rock; he was weak. He had failed. The man who no longer felt like a rock then did the only thing he was capable of doing – he went and hid in some unknown place as he broke down, weeping for the terrible thing he had done. He was not a leader of men; he had denied the one he believed had come from God. He was a miserable and detestable coward and failure!

"I am not a rock!"

While he wept in his solitary place, the one he had denied was nailed to a cross where he died. That night was terrible, as was the next day. The failed disciple could not bear to be there as the one sent from God hung on a cross. He could not bear to tell anybody what he had done. His shame consumed him and he could not forgive himself.

He wanted to stay away from everybody, but for the next few days he found comfort in being with other disciples. Like him, they were hiding from potential enemies who might want to arrest them, as they had arrested the one they had followed. The group of followers had difficulty talking with each other because they each knew they had failed the one they had followed for three years. They could not envision their life without the one sent from God.

On the third day, after the one from God had been killed, some women went to his burial place. To everyone's surprise they came back sooner than expected. They were filled with uncontrollable excitement as they babbled something incomprehensible at first and thoroughly unbelievable. What did they say?

"He is alive!"

"It can't be!"

"It is true! We have seen him. Alive!"

The women were chattering about angels, a rolled away stone, an empty tomb and seeing the one who spoke for God. The disciple who had been called Rock and another ran to go see for themselves. When they arrived at the burial tomb, there was no body in the tomb to be sure. Where did it go? There had to be some explanation. Could he be alive? If so, where was he now? Where was the one who came from God?

The women told the disciples that they had to go to Galilee where they would see the one who had come from God. As you can imagine, they did just that very thing as rapidly as possible. What was the shortest way? How light could they travel? Did they have to walk? Could they get rides and get there faster? Why was Samaria in the way? Such questions were irrelevant. They must get to Galilee and quickly, but they must also stay undetected in case enemies were looking for them.

When they finally arrived in Galilee, they found a secret place where they could meet and plot their course of action. Should they seek the one who came from God, or would he find them? They were not sure what to do. One Sunday evening, they sat around talking. All were there except for one. The door was locked for safety. As they discussed all that had transpired, the one sent from God suddenly appeared.

"He's alive!"

Indeed, he was alive. Joy of all joys! They laughed and shouted and celebrated. No longer did they cower in fear in that secret room. He was alive! They could see this with their own eyes. They could hear his voice with their own ears. They could touch him and embrace him, and be embraced by him.

Before the magnitude of the encounter could fully sink in, the miraculous reunion came to a sudden end. The one who came from God could not stay. He had to leave them for a while, but he would appear again to them when all of them were present. Each day after that held the hope that the one they followed would appear again.

It was wonderful for the disciple called Rock to see the one he believed in again but painful as well. How could he be with his risen Lord knowing what he had done? He had denied the one he claimed to believe in. What would his Lord want with him? The one who was from God never said anything to him about the events of that dark night that still haunted Rock, but he knew. The one from God had looked right at him when the rooster crowed. The man called Rock would never forget that look. What must his Lord think of him?

"I am no rock!"

Then it happened. The man called Rock and some of the disciples had gone fishing. At least they were trying to catch fish. Unfortunately, the fish did not want to be caught. They had fished all night and had nothing but aching backs and empty nets to show for it. Early in the morning, as the disciples rowed for shore, tired and discouraged, they saw a man standing on the bank. He shouted to them. What did he say? He was hard to hear at first.

"Throw your nets on the right side of the boat!"

The right side? All right. They did as they were instructed, and then the memories came rushing back into their awakened minds. This had happened once before. They caught more fish than they could pull into the boat. How could they not have recognized the man on the bank? It was the one who had come from God! Their leader had returned again. The man called Rock became so excited that he could not wait for the boat to get to shore. He just jumped right into the water and swam to shore.

When he got there, he was overjoyed to be there, but then again he wasn't. It was still awkward. What do you say to the one you denied? You cannot make small talk? How does one say, "I did not really mean it?" He had denied his Lord – not once, not twice but three times! The disciple called Rock did not know what to say, but the one from God knew what needed to be said to him.

"Rock, do you love me?"

"Yes, Lord, you know I love you!" His heart ached.

One time...

"Rock, do you love me?"

"Yes, Lord, you know I love you." He was in agony as he responded.

...two times...

"Rock, do you really love me?"

"Lord, you know everything. You know I love you." With all his heart, he yearned to take back his denials on that hated night. Why had he denied the one who came from God?

...three times!

Three times? Yes, three times, and so the disciple called Rock, was pulled back in by the tender touch of his Lord. He had done the unimaginable, the worst thing he could ever do. He had denied his Lord not once, not twice but three times. His Lord did not condemn him. Instead he had prayed for Rock, and now he reached out to him in order to affirm their relationship. He looked at this man he had named Rock and asked him, "Do you love me?" Not once, not twice but three times, and three times the answer came back, "You know I love you!" This new memory would conquer the one that had haunted Rock and empower him. From that day forward this disciple who had messed up so bad became a rock for his Lord. He became the leader of men that his Lord knew he could be. He lived a life that any man would aspire to, one that inspired others to live for a higher purpose, and he lived it with honor and valor. One day, the disciple called Rock would face again the possibility of dying for the one who had been sent from God. He would die before he would deny, and on that day, he lived up to his name.

In the times that have come and gone since, this man called Rock was not the only man in history to turn his back on the one who came from God. Others have done the same and needed the same opportunity to proclaim their renewed love for the one they have denied or deserted. The one who came from God has been speaking to them in countless ways through the centuries? He does that even now so that people may have an opportunity to turn back to him after turning their backs on him.

(The story of Peter is told throughout the gospels
of Matthew, Mark, Luke and John.)

"When they saw the courage of Peter and John and realized that they were unschooled, ordinary men, they took note that these men had been with Jesus. But since they could see the man who had been healed standing there with them, there was nothing they could say. So they ordered them to withdraw from the Sanhedrin and then conferred together. 'What are we going to do with these men?' they asked. 'Everybody living in Jerusalem knows they have done an outstanding miracle, and we cannot deny it. But to stop this thing from spreading any further among the people, we must warn these men to speak no longer to anyone in this name.'"
Then they called them in again and commanded them to not speak or teach at all in the name of Jesus. But Peter and John replied, "Judge for yourselves whether it is right in God's sight to obey you rather than God. For we cannot help speaking about what we have seen and heard."
Acts 4:13-20

Every man longs to do something significant in his life. There is no exception to this. What each man considers to be significant may vary, but the same desire resides within every man. Honor, courage, valor, bravery, strength, champion, victor...these are powerful words that call to each man. No man wants to be seen as a coward or a wimp. No man wants to be seen as weak. Men want to know that they have worked hard for something that was worthy of such efforts. They want to know they made a difference for the better in someone's life. They want to be respected and not taken for granted or dismissed.

Is there any higher calling to answer than the call of God? In what other pursuits can a man do something that will not only make a difference in people's lives for generations but forever? Just working for a paycheck, a bonus or a promotion pales in comparison. People were created for greater things than that. Why should men sit on the sidelines, or in their living rooms just drinking beer and cheering sports teams when they can be engaged in more noble and far greater contests themselves? What other pursuit will be worth all the effort a man will put forth over a lifetime?

Chapter 22

If he was angry, he had a right to be. If people had to be punished, so be it! He would stand with the council. No longer would lies be allowed to spread. This angry man had heard the stories about the man who claimed to speak for God. He knew that man had come to this Great City and had met his just end – executed, and rightly so, for he not only claimed to speak for God, he also claimed to be the Son of God. Such lies cannot be allowed. That man had paid for his lies with his life.

Now this angry man stood in the council and listened to another man claim that this executed man was not dead. He heard the witness claim that the executed man had been raised from the dead and that he truly was the Son of God. The council had been wrong to have him executed. Enough! They would hear no more, in fact, they could not stand to hear more.

"Take him away! Silence him! Kill him! Stone him!"

The result? A brave man was carried away and stoned while the angry man stood and watched with approval. This brave man became the first witness to die for the man who came from God. His sacrifice would not be forgotten, nor would the angry man ever forget his part in the witness' death.

This brave witness would not be the last one to die. The angry man would see to that. He would make it his mission to stomp out this lie by persecuting those who believed in the one they claimed was alive again. He would kill, arrest, jail and do everything legally conceivable to squash this lie. The angry man marched out day after day, trip after trip, with orders from the council, granting him unrestricted authority to arrest anyone who claimed to believe in the one said to be raised from the dead. This angry man put many believers in jail for their stubborn belief in that man.

Even though he did not like these people, he could not help but notice their bravery and peaceful spirit at the time of their arrests. The angry man could not understand why they so willingly suffered so much for a man who was dead. How could a lie have such a strong hold on a person's heart? He would show them no quarter because they blasphemed his God by proclaiming this executed man was the Son of God. They did not deserve mercy.

The angry man became both champion and enemy at the same time. For those who opposed this new belief, like those on the council, he was their champion. They loved him and honored him. They gave him anything he desired. He would be the instrument that would finally quell the rebellion and silence the lie. For those who believed in the one who was raised from the dead, he was an enemy. They feared him; they tried to avoid him. Who could count the friends and family members they knew who had suffered at the hands of this angry man?

If you look closer, you will notice that the people who favored him were those who had power. On the other hand, his enemies had no positions of power, no armies to fight for them. They were weak and vulnerable. The angry man knew that these liars and deceivers would be defeated. This was inevitable.

Still you must look even closer. You must discover the truth underneath all the turmoil. Did the ones who were arrested and killed really base their beliefs on a lie? If so then the angry young man was correct, but if not, the greater power did not side with this angry man. If that were the case, what was inevitable would be far different from what that man expected.

One day the inevitable happened. The angry man went on one of his trips to arrest another cluster of believers. As he neared his destination, a brilliant light, more intense than the sun, struck him down. The force of the light overwhelmed him, and he lay stunned on the ground. Then he heard a voice speak to him and call him by name:

"Why do you persecute me?"

"Persecute who? Whose voice is this?" said the angry man.

"I am Jesus."

"Jesus?"

It could not be. He was dead. Impossible! Yet, as he lay there on the ground trembling at the power in the voice that spoke like God, he knew it had to be true. This was terrible, for if Jesus was not dead this angry man was in trouble! That meant Jesus truly did speak for God. It meant that he truly was the Son of God, and that meant the angry man had been opposing God all along!

What would happen to him now? Would the Son of God strike him down as he had struck down others? That would be a fitting judgment; now he understood that he deserved no less. He tried to look at the voice that spoke to him, but something was wrong. He could not see. He was blind!

The voice of the living Jesus spoke to him again.

"Get up and go into town. I will tell you later what will happen to you."

What choice did the blind and frightened man have? He was no longer angry. If anyone had a right to be angry it would be the one he had been persecuting, the one who had struck him down on the road. Now blind, he found himself trembling in uncertainty and fear. He had been wrong about this executed man and his followers. His fate surely was sealed; he had only to wait for the sentence to be pronounced. The light disappeared when the voice of Jesus stopped speaking, and the blind and frightened man's companions led him into town where he stayed for several days.

What would he do while he waited? He did not know. He had never been in this situation before. This certainly was the first time he had been blind. More than that, he had never questioned the correctness of his actions before. Now, without question, he knew he could not have been more wrong in his actions. If blindness was his only punishment, it would be no less than fair, even if he remained blind for the rest of his life. His physical blindness reflected how blind he had been to the truth before his encounter on the road. He now faced with great uncertainty the unfolding of his immediate future. The blind and frightened man knew of nothing else to do but pray to the Son of God that he had persecuted. He prayed for three solid days.

Then the Son of God sent another man, one of his followers, to go see the praying man. This follower was frightened because he had heard many stories about this angry man that he had been instructed to meet. He did not know that this man was now praying to the same Lord as he. Nevertheless, this fearful man obeyed his Lord and went to see the praying man. As he met with the praying blind man, he gave him the message the Son of God told him to give.

"You will now speak for me. I will send you to faraway places, and you will suffer much for me, just as you have caused others to suffer. Now get up and be baptized and have your sins washed away."

What did the praying man think when he heard these words? He heard what he had been called to do, but was that what mattered most to him at the moment? Perhaps what mattered most were the words that set him free from his past of persecuting believers. If he were to be baptized, his sins would be washed away. Instead of judgment, he had received a mission and a way to forgiveness. Could it be true? Would he be given a second chance? He would never forget how the one he persecuted had shown him mercy. He gladly received it as well as the mission he had been given by the one he now willingly served. Immediately, he got up and was baptized. As he rose out of the water, two marvelous things occurred. Who can say which one he valued most? He could see again, and he was free of all of his past actions that now shamed him!

An angry man had become a blind and frightened man. The blind and frightened man had become a praying man, and that praying man had become a new man, God's man. He soon found others in the city who believed in the resurrected man from God. He had come to arrest them so he did not know if they would welcome him. The disciple who had baptized him introduced this former enemy to other believers. This former enemy shared with those disciples a message about the God who gives people second chances.

At first, they were afraid to be with this new man. This was only natural. They did not know if this man could be trusted. Was his conversion real or simply a new tactic that would help him arrest more believers? Soon they realized he truly had become one of them, and when this new man's life was threatened, they gladly helped their friend escape. For a while, the man seemed to disappear, and no one heard from him or about him.

You may wonder what happened to this new man, but if you look closer, you will see that something necessary had to occur. The new man of God had gone to a place to learn more from the God who had spoken to him on the road and who had called him by name. He was being prepared for his mission, the one given to him on the road that fateful day. This man of God would soon go speak the words of God to people who had never heard them before. The mission would last his lifetime, and he would have to endure unthinkable suffering. Eventually, this mission would require not just his life but also his death. Now you know the truth as to why this man of God needed time to prepare.

The time arrived for this chosen man to go on his mission. Where would his Lord send him? What would be his first destination? The possibilities were endless because this new faith was primarily centered in one region. There were countless masses spread across the nations who still had heard nothing of the God this man now served. The man had been prepared and was ready to go wherever his Lord sent him.

Then the man of God learned something about the God he now served: expect the unexpected. The Lord told him to go back to the city where it all began, back to where the council was. He had to go back to the Great City, back to the place where his terrible memories lay. He had to go back to the place where he had taken part in killing the brave witness. Why back there? He would prefer to go anywhere but there. However, his Lord called him to go there, and that was where he would go. He had no choice.

At first, he had great difficulty in meeting with the believers. None trusted him and every one of them avoided him in spite of his best efforts. Some may have heard stories of his conversion, but he had since disappeared. No one knew what to expect from him. Then an encouraging man entered into his life. This fellow believer met with him and talked with him. He saw that this was indeed a new man, a man chosen to do great and important things for the risen Lord. This encourager took this chosen man to meet with the leaders and the other believers.

Always in the back of this chosen man's mind though was the brave witness. He would never forget him. Even though he never threw a stone, he had helped kill a good man. What would he say if he met the brave witness' family? Did the witness have a wife who was now a widow because of him? Did he have children that were now fatherless because of him? Even though he was a single man, this chosen man's heart was broken by what he had done. He would live the rest of his days wishing he could undo that one day's events, and many other days as well.

Yet, the chosen man had come to know the grace of a God who specializes in giving people second chances. He would spend his life telling others his story, but more importantly, he would spend his life telling the story of the risen Jesus. He would speak with people who also had made mistakes, to other people who would need second chances. Many people would come to know Jesus and call him Lord just as the chosen man now did. They would follow in the same steps he did and would be baptized to have their sins washed away. They, too, would become new. They, too, would do great and important things for their Lord.

Perhaps the brave witness did have a wife and children, and maybe they met this chosen man in that Great City where this chapter of his story was written. If so, that part of the story is not revealed to us. Does it need to be? Is not the story also about us and the second chances that we need? We need the same mercy. Perhaps we need God to call out to us as we head down our own roads of self-destruction. Maybe we need to be given a new calling for our lives, and perhaps we also will meet again those who have been greatly wronged at our hands. If that happens, we will realize it was not just about what God did for this chosen man back then, but what he will do for us in our moment in time. At such times, we will discover the true power of God's mercy and how grateful we are for a second chance.

Our imaginations can fill out the story when we think of the meeting between the chosen man and the family of the brave witness. Our response when we hear the voice of the God who gives second chances will determine what is written on the pages of our stories. We will live out those pages.

(This biblical story is found in Acts 9, 22 and 26.)

"What shall we say then? Shall we go on sinning so that grace may increase? By no means! We died to sin; how can we live it in any longer? Or don't you know that all of us who were baptized into Christ Jesus were baptized into his death? We were therefore buried with him through baptism into death in order that, just as Christ was raised from the dead through the glory of the Father, we too may live a new life." "What benefit did you reap at that time from the things you are now ashamed of? Those things result in death! But now that you have been set free from sin and have become slaves to God, the benefit you reap leads to holiness, and the result is eternal life. For the wages of sin is death, but the gift of God is eternal life in Christ Jesus our Lord. Romans 6:1-4, 21-23

Some words pack power. The power of some words can debilitate and kill. These words have power to change the course of a life forever, power to drive a person into darkness so black that life will be suffocated within it. Guilt. Shame. These are two such words.

Have you ever wondered why disciples of Jesus are baptized? For one reason, it is through their baptism that they proclaim to all that Jesus is their Lord and that they live for God. However, their baptism is also something they need. Every single one of them carries the guilt of doing wrong, sometimes unknowingly, often times with full knowledge and awareness. They know the dreadful power of shame. They need a second chance, and they seize it when it is offered.

These are the ones who hear God and respond to his call. Guilt and shame belong to their past, not their present or their future. They are not ashamed of God, and God is not ashamed of them. They are new, they are free and they are loved.

Chapter 23

If you read the Bible long enough you will find yourself somewhere in its pages. That is what you can expect when you pick up a book written by God. He had this book written so that people everywhere can find themselves in it. When you pick it up and read it, know that God speaks to you. He has a message that comes from his heart to yours so when you read of someone else's story and find your heart stirring, perhaps it is your story, too.

Sometimes it is a story of bravery that catches your breath. Sometimes one of despair moves you to tears. At some point in time, every reader has the opportunity to find themselves in a story of redemption. As one of those readers, you might find yourself in the story of a father and his child, a son that the he loved very much. It matters not if you are a son or a daughter, still a child or grown, or whether or not you have a good father. The story is powerful enough to speak to every longing heart.

Normally, a child does not get an inheritance until the father has died, and most children do not look forward to the day. Few would dream of speeding its coming, but can you imagine a selfish and impatient child in a rush for that day to come just so he could claim his inheritance? What would you think of such a child? If you can imagine such a son and feel the emotions rising within you then you can transport yourself into the story told once by the one who speaks for God. You are now an invisible observer who watches the story unfold. As it does, you become emotionally attached to the father and the son. You begin to feel what they must have felt.

As the story goes, a particular young man was feeling his oats and could not wait to live his own life, to be his own man. He had grown tired of living in his father's house and living by his father's rules. He wanted to make his own rules. He did not want to answer to anybody anymore so one day he went to his father and demanded his inheritance.

"Give it to me. I want it now!"

He might as well have said to his father, "You are dead to me now!"

It is not every day that a father is confronted with such a demand from his son. We might be tempted to simply dismiss the remarks of the young man if not for the devastating blow it laid on the father's heart. How is a father supposed to respond to his son after such a demand? What would you expect the father to say? Would it surprise you to know that the father did not say anything? Perhaps it would surprise you even more to find out the father actually gave his son the inheritance he demanded.

"Why would he do this? Does the father not understand that he is not supposed to reward selfishness?"

The reason for the father's response is really very simple. The father did not want his son to stay if his son did not want to be with him. Oh, he loved his son and wanted him to stay, but the father was not going to force his son to love him. Because he loved his son, he did the only thing he could do – the father gave his son the inheritance he demanded and let him go.

This selfish son was overjoyed to be free. Now he could live his life the way he wanted. He did not have to worry about curfews or about someone checking up on him. He did not have to give reasons for anything he did, and he did not have to answer any questions regarding his behavior. He was a man, and he could do well enough on his own. He did not need his father anymore.

The young man journeyed as far away from his father as he could. If he were going to get a new start, he did not need to worry about word getting back to his father. He sure did not want to live in fear of his father sending someone after him. Freedom could only be found as far away as possible from the one he had answered to all his life.

Not only did freedom mean he had to be far away from his father, it also meant he would do what his father would not approve. To be his own man, he had to be different. How different? He would do just the opposite of his father. He would hang with a different type of people and find pleasure in things that his father would think disgusting. He would spend his money freely on pleasure instead of managing it like some foolish old man like his father. He would not worry about work and earning money. He had plenty! The young man would take each day as it came, giving no thought to the morrow. This was freedom. This was being his own man. This was the life!

Now, some might think this young man had the best life possible. You might even agree. The young man certainly thought so, and in his eyes, he had no reason to look back. What could be so bad about doing what you want, when you want, as often as you want, with whomever you wanted? For the young man, as it is with many others like him, there was nothing wrong with that. However, everything that glitters is not gold, as they say, and the young man would soon discover this hard truth. What was new and exciting gradually became quite old and very boring, even tiresome. As the thrill and rush diminished, he went to greater and greater extremes to experience the same level of pleasure and ecstasy.

The days became darker for the young man as he turned a corner that he had not anticipated. He plunged even deeper into the new lifestyle that he had freely chosen. Now he did things that not only would disgust his father but disgusted him as well. To cover his disgust, he sought ways to deaden his feelings. He needed no conscience for the new life he had chosen. He just needed the next pleasure, but that pleasure was like a wind that he could never catch.

As he chased those winds, he watched his inheritance slip unstoppably through his fingers. His reckless lifestyle had nearly bankrupted him financially, and worse yet, morally. He cared not so much about the latter condition, but in order to sustain his new life, he had to change his habits. However, changing the habits of his liberated life was not easy. Those habits had already become engrained in his still selfish heart. The young man found that he could not change. Truthfully, he really did not want to, because he did not want to become like his father. He wanted to be his own man and live the life he had chosen for himself, so he kept on.

What feelings do you have for the young man now? Do you feel disgust? Maybe you believe he got what he deserved as you feel your anger towards him vindicated. Perhaps you find yourself second guessing the young man as you contemplate how you would have spent your inheritance were you in his shoes. Maybe, you just feel sadness for the young man. Emotions run deep in such a story.

As the story continues, the young man kept on in his lifestyle until his money was no longer his. It was gone. Others had his money now, and he found himself penniless and destitute. Still, he reckoned he had nothing to fear. When he had money to burn, he had spent it freely on his friends, and now they would surely take care of him. The young man did not worry because his friends would prove true. That is when he found out that he did not have any friends. Those who had claimed to be his friends when he had money could hardly be found now, and if he did find them, they had no time for his problems. They did not want to deal with this wretched young man who no longer could spend money on them. They never liked him in the first place. He chose this life; let him live with it now.

How long had it taken the young man to reach such a sorry state? It seemed like a lifetime. When he thought back to his old life at home with his father, he felt he was snatching glimpses of a different man in a different world. He had become a stranger to himself now. He did not look like the young man who had left his father's home. His face looked older than his years; his body seemed old as well. Hard living had taken its toll on him. Most likely, no one at home would even recognize him now. He did not even recognize himself when he saw his reflection.

What should he do? What could he do? He could not stay where he was. He could not go back home. He had to find a way to survive or die on the streets. Slowly starving to death terrified the young man. In order to avoid that fate, he did what he had never, ever thought he would do. He was ashamed to do it, but it was all he could do, and it was the only work available to him. It was the only way he could get some money to feed his hungry belly. He took a job slopping pigs and taking care of their needs!

This job was so frowned upon by his community that no decent, honorable person would ever do it. Decency and honor had been no concern of his for such a long time, but now the young man choked on those ideas in his debased state. Like the pigs he tended, he was filthy and disgusting.

Stronger than his disgust for himself was his desire to eat. The man he worked for did not pay the young man enough to live on. He was a cruel and heartless employer who cared nothing for the young man's welfare. In order to stave off hunger, the young man would eat any food available to him, including the food he gave daily to the pigs. Even as the stench filled his nostrils, his mouth watered for the slop that could fill his belly.

How could he have sunken so low? What had brought him to this point? He knew the answer, but he did not like to think about it because he was the answer. He wallowed in this sorry state because he had chosen this life. True enough, he did not know his life would turn out like it did, but he was the one who made the choices all the way.

"What have I done?"

He was in this sorry, pitiful state because he had put himself there. He had received what he deserved, and he deserved no better.

At some point you become so lost that you have to do something drastic. Some people reach that point, and they end the tragedy in their lives by some tragic means. Their life has become dark and their thinking even darker. They see no other way out. They know they cannot continue as they are because it will only get worse. They escape the pain the only way they can see. They take their own life.

There are others who reach that point who do not wish to end their lives of misery. Some may think they are afraid to pull the trigger, take the jump or swallow the pills. These people may even convince themselves that they are cowards who cannot do the one courageous thing left. Yet that is not true, for no matter how much misery envelopes them, they still have some whisper of hope to which they desperately cling. Or perhaps it is that faint hope that clings to them, calling out to them from distant memories. This last little bit of hope is their way out of a death trap. It is their lifeline.

When this wretched young man reached that point in his life, instead of reaching for a rope or a knife, he reached for a lifeline. This lifeline was the memory of his past. Memories that he had been running from now drew him back. He thought of his previous life and how good it really was.

"How could I have been so blind? Why did I give it all up? If only I could do it all over again!"

Then it occurred to him, he *could* do it all over again, in a way. He could go back home and tell his father that he wanted to come back. He wanted so badly to go back, but would his father even allow his return?

"I will tell my father that I know I can't be loved as a son again, but please take me back as a servant."

Perhaps he could do that. It would mean he would have to humble himself, and he would probably have to grovel at his father's feet. It probably would mean that he would get the worse jobs that could be thrown his way, but it would mean getting out of his current mess. Nothing could be worse than where he was. He could clean up on the outside, and maybe over time, he could clean up on the inside as well. At the very least, no matter how humiliated and ashamed he would feel, he would always have plenty of food. That he knew.

With that thought driving him, the starving, wretched young man who had made a mess of his life through one poor choice after another swallowed his pride and followed his only lifeline back home. With no trace of pride or self-esteem left, he stumbled resolutely back to face the man who scared him more than anyone else in the world – his father. He was afraid his father would say no, and more afraid that he would say yes. He was afraid of the other things his father would say before he said yes or no. He was afraid, but this was his last little bit of hope, and so he had to go home.

This brings us back to the father. Before the son comes home, we should consider what the father has been doing since his son left. It might surprise you. You may think that once his son left, the father grieved a little bit and moved on with his life, if he grieved at all. He certainly would not be wrong if he did not miss a son who had been so selfish and disrespectful towards him. Why should he lose one minute of sleep over a son that had chosen a different life than the one he offered? Had he not worked hard to give his son the best? Why should he care about a selfish son who had rejected all of that? You might think that this father was that sort of father, but you would be wrong.

The truth is that this father had never stopped thinking about his son that was now lost to him. His love for his son ran deep, and every morning he longed to hear his son's voice calling out to him. Every night he went to bed hoping that tomorrow would be the day his son would come back. When he slept at night he dreamed of all the good times he had with his son, back when his son was happy. How he would love to just get one letter from his son so that he would know his son was safe.

Frequently he thought about that day his son had demanded his inheritance. Perhaps he should have refused. Would it have been wiser to force his son to stay instead of allowing his son to act on his foolishness? A big part of him wished that he had done that, but in his heart, he knew he had done the only thing a father who loved his son could do. If he had any hope of his son one day freely loving him, he had to let him go. That was the most painful thing the father had ever done in his life and the absolute worst day of his life. Yet, if he could re-live that day, he would not do anything different. Love can be tough on a father.

Would you care to take a moment and consider your feelings for the father now? Sorrow? Is pity too strong of a word? Feelings and emotions run deep in such a story as this.

Not unexpectedly, the father never wished his son bad. He had hoped his son's life would go well. He did not want his son to struggle or to fail. He did not want him to be hurt. Even though he hoped that good would come his son's way, he knew his son, and he knew what his son's heart was set on. Even as he wished his son well, he knew it would not be so. The father could only hope that his son was safe, and that one day, he would come back home. That was the father's only hope, but as each day passed, his hope grew dimmer. He would not stop hoping though because, as a father, he had to hang on. This was his only lifeline to his son. He could not give up.

Now you know the fathers' heart. You know the son is on the way home, and so you know something the father doesn't know yet. As an invisible observer, you find yourself biting your lip so that you do not say anything. You wait and watch for the son's imminent return. You see the father wandering about absent-mindedly. You realize his thoughts are far away, in some distant, unknown land where his son lives. You watch as the father repeatedly looks out the window to see if anyone is coming. You notice that he jumps with anticipation every time he hears a voice outside. You know whose voice he longs to hear. You understand why his heart sinks a little lower with each disappointment. You think that if the son does not come back soon perhaps the father's heart could never be happy again. The damage may be too great and the scars too deep.

As you watch the father wait, you find yourself becoming more anxious. You are drawn more into the unfolding drama as your heart aches with the father's.

"Why is the son taking so long?"

"Has he gotten lost?"

"Has something terrible happened to him since we last saw him?"

You begin to worry about the son, too. You begin to understand a little of how the father has felt every day since his son disappeared out of sight. How did the father stand the strain? If the son only knew how much his father loved him, he would have never left.

"How could anybody walk away from a father who loved him so much?"

You force yourself to stop asking questions so that you can watch the father. He busies himself with mindless things. He has not been able to think about anything except his lost son for years. Some days are worse than others, but there is never a good day away from his son. The father walks out the door and sits on the porch just so he can keep an eye out. He sits and waits. He keeps a steady gaze down the road. He looks as far as he can see, until the road disappears over the hill. He strains to see any movement at all. He has done this every day. He sits for hours, looking down this road, but every day for the past several years, he has always gone back into the house broken-hearted.

He lets out a heavy sigh. His son is not coming home today. Perhaps tomorrow will be the day. He gets up and starts to turn back towards the door.

"What was that?"

Was that something moving down the road that he had seen out of the corner of his eye? He looks back. No, it is just shadows as the sun begins to set. His old eyes were just playing tricks on him.

"There it is again! It isn't the shadows. It *is* something moving. No, it is *someone* walking down the road!"

The father looks intently down the road. Who could this person be? It looks like no one he has ever seen. It must be some stranger traveling by, but something about this person looks vaguely familiar, even from this great distance. He watches closely, looking for anything he can remember. This person walks strangely. He walks so hesitantly. Each step seems to be harder to take and slower to fall. One would think this person did not want to come this way at all.

As the father watches, his heart begins to beat faster and faster. His breathing comes more rapidly. Almost without notice, tears start to stream down his face. His hope starts to rise up. There is something familiar about this person. It does not matter how many years have passed, a father recognizes his son anywhere! As soon as recognition sets in, the father begins shouting.

"My son has come home! My son has come home!"

The father bolted off the porch of his house and ran madly down the road. He did not know his old legs could run so fast. He sees his son stop as he runs toward him. Then the father sees his son reach out his arms and run towards him.

"My son is running home to me! Can you believe it? My son is running home to me!"

Finally, they are in each other's arms. The father is weeping uncontrollably for his lost son that he now holds safely in his arms. The son weeps uncontrollably in the safety of those arms. How could he have ever left? Perhaps as you find yourself watching this father and son you, too, wipe a tear from your cheek.

The son tries to beg his father for just a servant's place in the servants' quarters, but he is not able to speak. His father is shouting out commands to everyone.

"Quick, bring me the best robe for my son. He is my son! I have to get him out of these filthy rags. Where is my ring? Bring me my ring! I must give it to my son. Hurry! My son is home. Get a feast prepared. We are going to celebrate tonight. Hurry! Hurry! My son is home."

The son speaks up again, "Father, please listen. You don't understand. I have done horrible things. I am no longer worthy to be your son. Just let me be a…"

The son never gets to finish though. His father puts his hands on his son's shoulders and looks him in the eyes as joyous tears fall.

"You are my son. I have always loved you. Nothing could ever change that. I will always love you. You are my son. Welcome home!"

Thus we leave the father and son at the party, both happy to be in each other's company once more. We know that will never change. The son is home for good. Now it is time for us to leave them and enter into our own lives again. Yet, we never really leave them for what was just a story Jesus told about a father and son is more than that. People who have read this story throughout time have found themselves in this universal story. Every person can find himself or herself in it, every man or woman, boy or girl, whether old or young. Perhaps you have, as well. All of us have been the lost child at some point in our lives. All of us can see the young man in ourselves.

(This biblical story is found in Luke 15.)

"We must pay more careful attention,
therefore, to what we have heard,
so that we do not drift away.
For if the message spoken by angels was binding,
and every violation and disobedience
received its just punishment,
how shall we escape if we ignore such a great salvation?
This salvation, which was first announced by the Lord,
was confirmed to us by those who heard him.
Hebrews 2:1-3

Some of us are home. Some of us are still in that far off land hanging on to that last little whisper of hope. That hope is a lifeline that can lead each one back to the Father. There is no life, no child that is not precious to him. If you are that lost child, off in some far distant country, follow your lifeline back home. Hear your Father say to you, "You are my child. I have always loved you. There is nothing you have ever done that could change that. You are my child. Come home. I am waiting to welcome you with tears and open arms."

Epilogue

How far away is heaven? How many miles span the distance between heaven and earth? These are childhood questions that we stop asking because we have no answer. Yet, the distance between heaven and earth can be considered in terms other than miles. For instance, how great is the distance between a perfect world and a world corrupted and scarred by sin and death? How great is the distance between a holy God and people twisted by evil? Could we measure that?

Or we could ask how much distance God's Son had to cover in order to live among us? What was it like for Jesus to interact with humans instead of angels? We might consider it a terrible adjustment, going from associating with angels to associating with people, especially when we recall the "worst of us" that we all know. Many of us choose not to associate with such people because they are too disagreeable or too unlikable or too...whatever. If we, who are corrupted, find such people intolerable, how could a holy God associate with them? Uncomfortably, we move from thinking about the "worst of us" to remembering the "worst in us." How could a holy God associate with us? The chasm between his holiness and our sinfulness is so great. As difficult as we may think it might have been for Jesus to cross that distance, he seems to have found it fairly easy to fall in love with us – even the worst of us. Isn't that amazing?

How far did Jesus have to go to hang out with a woman who had been married five times and who lived with a man not her husband? How far did he have to go to enter the home of a corrupt tax collector? Or to spend part of his day with an adulterous woman? How far did God have to go to enter a bar owned by a small woman and frequented by an assortment of hurting and broken people? How far did he have to go to be with any of the people in these stories? How far do God and Jesus have to go to be with any one of us?

When we stop to consider how far God had to go to reach us and the great lengths to which his son, Jesus, had to go in order to reach us, truth hits hard. It is incredible that they would even do so. Yet, their willingness to do this is beyond question. Because God and his son made that remarkable journey, the great distance between us has been spanned. They did it uninvited, and for the most part, they were unwelcome. To the vast majority of people who have lived on this earth since, their effort has gone unappreciated.

The efforts of God and Jesus raise a more important question for us to consider: how far are we willing to go to be with God? God speaks to us in various ways so that we would go to him. How will we respond to his call?

It is not surprising that God calls out to us. We may be shocked to find that God goes to some of the places in life that we frequent just so he can speak to us. We may be ashamed to have been found in such places. However, where we are when God speaks to us is not as important as us whether or not we hear the voice that calls and go to him who calls us. Will we leave behind the darkness and embrace the light? We all have a "barstool" of some sort that we need to leave behind.

We all have our own stories, and God has spoken into each one. You have heard some of the story of a preacher, of a small woman who owned a bar and the people who walked through the door of that bar. You have heard ancient stories of others who have long since died. Now, at this place and time, you live out and write yours. However, you do not write it alone because God has some say in every story – even yours. Chapters still have to be written, you have many pages still to turn, but your story will eventually have an ending. How will it end?

"This is the verdict: Light has come into the world, but men loved darkness instead of light because their deeds were evil. Everyone who does evil hates the light, and will not come into the light for fear that his deeds will be exposed. But whoever lives by the truth comes into the light, so that it may be seen plainly that what he has done has been done through God."
John 3:19-21

A Final Word

I have not written this book just for people who like to go to churches, although all who desire are welcome to read it. I hope it is the kind of book that will help people from all walks of life, but I have written especially for the people who don't often go to churches, whatever the reason may be. I hope this book finds a place in the hearts of people whose lives have been turned upside down and who have lost their way. I realize that no one likes to be told they are lost, but don't we all lose our way at some point? There is no shame in feeling lost; the tragedy is in staying lost.

I have shared with you stories about real people, some I have met in my life, and some I have read about in the Bible. If you have not had much of a relationship with God, or any at all, my hope is that as you have read about these people, you realized this great and loving God is trying to speak to you. Has he indeed spoken to you? Absolutely. Is he still doing so? Without a doubt. How so? It is not as mysterious as it may seem, and more than anyone else, you can see this, if you will look. Your story may have been difficult, even tragic, so far, but God has been there to carry you through. He is keenly interested in how your story will continue. He wants to help you write more than a happy ending. He wants your whole life to be one of blessings with every page touched by his love. How your story unfolds depends upon how you respond to the God who speaks to you.

I truly desire that the telling of these stories awakens a desire in the hearts of every reader to read the Bible. This unique book that we call the Bible not only tells you about people like yourself, it tells you about the God who is real. It is truly an incredible gift from God. The storyline of the Bible is not hard to understand. God loves you, and he will do anything he can to show you that love. He hopes that you will love him back. He gave us his recorded word so that we may know how to do that. I have tried to faithfully share that with you in these stories.

I hope the book I have penned helps each of you who picks it up to realize that you have a story to tell as well. It may not seem interesting to you, but your story is important and special, unique enough to need telling. There are people, still far away from the God who loves them, who need to hear how God has touched your life. Perhaps this book will ignite a fire within you and spur you on to share your story with them. Prayerfully pass a copy of this book to someone who needs to know this awesome God. Write a personal note to them somewhere in the front. When the time is right, share from the pages of your own life where God has been writing. You may start at the beginning, or you may start somewhere in the middle. Wherever you start, it will be a story worth telling because God helped you pen it. If sharing these stories emboldens you and helps you share your own then I am grateful. In a world where so many people have lost their way, more people need to proclaim the stories of how God has been speaking to them. May God bless the telling of your story!

Kerruso

In the beginning was the Word, and
the Word was with God,
and the Word was God. He was
with God in the beginning.
Through him all things were made;
without him nothing was made that has been made.
In him was life, and that life was the light of men.
The light shines in the darkness, but the
darkness has not understood it...
Yet to all who received him, to those
who believed in his name,
he gave the right to become children of God —
children born not of natural descent, nor of
human decision or a husband's will,
but born of God.
The Word became flesh and made his dwelling among us.
We have seen his glory, the glory of the One and Only,
who came from the Father, full of grace and truth.
John 1:1-5, 12-14

CPSIA information can be obtained
at www.ICGtesting.com
Printed in the USA
FFOW03n1447150118
44572110-44414FF

9 781512 732610